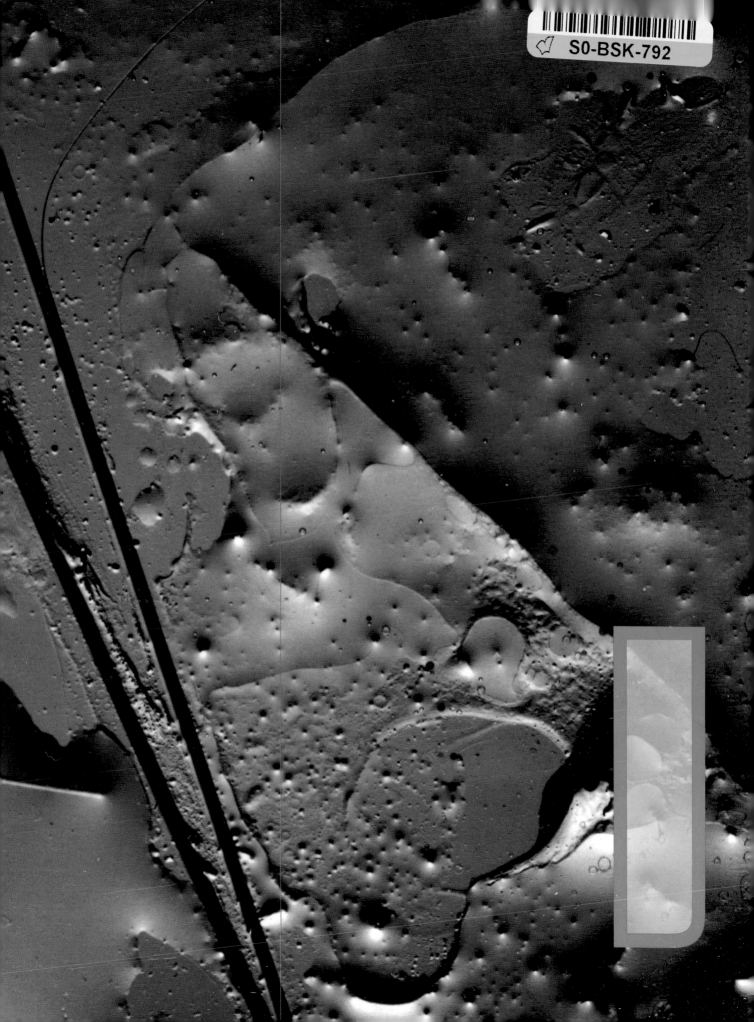

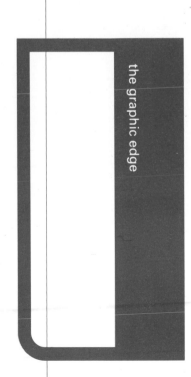

the graphic edge

Booth-Clibborn Editions, London

Design by Sean Perkins

the graphic edge

rick poynor

First published in 1993
by Booth-Clibborn Editions
12 Percy Street
London W1P 9FB

Reprinted November 1993

Printed and bound in Hong Kong
by Dai Nippon Printing Co.

Copyright ©1993 Rick Poynor

ISBN 1873968 078

Published and distributed
in the United Kingdom.
Direct mail rights in Europe:
Internos Books
12 Percy Street
London W1P 9FB
England

Distributors for the rest of the world:
Hearst Books International
1350 Avenue of the Americas
New York NY 10019
United States of America

Distributed to the book trade and art trade
in the United States and Canada by:
North Light Books,
an imprint of F&W Publications, Inc.
1507 Dana Avenue
Cincinnati, Ohio 45207
United States of America

Book design: Sean Perkins
Design assistance: Wendelin Hess
Concept photography: Richard J. Burbridge
Project photography: Gareth McCarthy
Editorial assistance: Liz Farrelly

Acknowledgements

Thanks to Why Not Associates, Vicky Wilson,
Gerard Forde, Phoa Kia Boon, Williams and
Phoa, Adrian Caddy, Imagination, Carl Mooney,
Alan Drew, Vancouver Art Gallery, Lawrence
Weiner, Warner Books

Notes from the edge This book has been conceived as a companion volume to an earlier book, *Typography Now: The Next Wave*. It is not a "part two" in the Hollywood sense in which an original idea becomes progressively thinner with each sequel or remake. Instead, it attempts to cover ground which the earlier book, by definition, could not examine. I should make it clear at the outset that this is not a book specifically about typography, or for that matter about a specific kind of typography. Hardly any of the work included is wholly typographic in content and examples of new typefaces are not shown, except where they feature as an integral part of a design. *The Graphic Edge*, as its title suggests, is a book about graphic design. It acknowledges the stylistic and expressive possibilities of the new digital typography, but argues the need at this point to go beyond the letterform as an end in itself and to reassess the ways in which word and image can interact to create graphic meaning. What this collection does share with *Typography Now* is a desire to piece together and begin to make sense of work by designers who in many cases choose to operate at the edge of the profession, or at the very least to distance themselves from the commercial mainstream. In the spirit of the work itself, this is a highly personal selection rather than the official conclusion of a jury or committee, but one that has been made with the journalistic and critical aim of showing new developments and trying to pin down that elusive phenomenon, the contemporary mood. It concentrates on work that looks of its time and which in the long view stands a good chance of coming to define the visual landscape of its time. In other words, it explores the characteristics that make the graphic design of the early 1990s different from what has gone before. These editorial aims mean that much else that is interesting or worthwhile, but less overtly concerned with formal and structural experiment, has been excluded. Other categories of graphic design are better dealt with at the proper length elsewhere.

The designs collected here, with a handful of exceptions, come from Great Britain, the United States and the Netherlands. Almost all of them were executed in the 1990s. They are divided into four thematic categories – "Cool", "Layered", "Conceptual" and "Raw" – intended to exemplify recent trends. As with any attempt at classification, the categories are not always mutually exclusive. There are many designs that could be included in only one category, but there are others that would fit reasonably smoothly into two or sometimes three categories. In such cases, classification has been determined by the characteristics that seem the most salient, and by the design's relationship to other pieces less ambiguously placed in the same category. It would have been possible to continue to break down categories until the book was divided into ten or more sections. Within the "Raw" section, for instance, I might have separated hand-drawn letterforms from machine generated typeforms. My purpose, however, was not to achieve a detailed taxonomy of graphic styles so much as a broad sequence of representative moods and themes. The editing and arrangement of designs within a given category should help to

reveal connections, confluences and contrasts of style and approach without the need for explicit division and labelling.

The category titles are intended to be self-explanatory, but before going on to a more general discussion I will offer some brief definitions. In the work included in the "Cool" category, compositional frameworks tend to be open and uncluttered, with white space showing through; pictorial elements are relatively simple and bold. Sans serif typefaces are preferred, though not obligatory, and much of the work shows clear signs of descent from earlier Swiss models. In "Layered", on the other hand, type and imagery are woven into compositions of much greater intricacy and congestion. In the most contorted and baroque examples, the design is saturated with visual and verbal information, leaving the viewer to decide what is most important and where to begin. The choice of typefaces is more varied and there is frequent use of the quirkier computer fonts. Stylistically many of the designs in "Conceptual" bear a resemblance to those in "Cool", but the work has a more personal and at times enigmatic quality; it is the kind of design most likely to be accused of

Photographic studies showing how
words influence our reading of an image
Project set by Dan Friedman
Designer: Stuart Friedman
Yale University
USA, 1992

"There are two kinds of light – the glow that illuminates,
and the glare that obscures." *James Thurber*

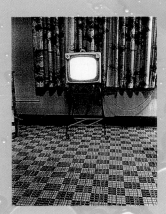  

masquerading as art. There are signs of influence
from the art world in the use of type on image and
some of the projects have in fact been created for
artists or exhibitions. Sometimes this leads to poetic
mystification, sometimes it results in work of unusual
penetration and rigour. The designs in "Raw" are
equally personal, but the effect is less cerebral and the
level of formal idiosyncrasy much higher. This is the
least "designerly" work: spontaneity is preferred to
detachment, rough edges to professional finish,
emotional expression to suffocating good taste.

    Typography Now was criticised for showing
such a high proportion of work from what might be
described as the cultural arena, and the same thing
could doubtless be said of this collection. The reason
for this emphasis is simple: if you go looking for
experimentation, this is where you tend to find it.
The implication of the criticism is that a design
approach is somehow only valid if it presupposes,
and addresses itself to, the widest possible audience.
Despite the proliferating evidence to the contrary, the
idea of "universality" in graphic design dies hard.
A distinction is also drawn, sometimes explicitly,
between the supposedly esoteric domain of culture –

inhabited by whom? culture vultures? – and the
so-called "real" world inhabited by the rest of us.
This is a very peculiar and divisive view of culture and
one that bears little relation to what happens in
reality. All kinds of people watch films, visit the theatre,
read books and magazines, listen to records, and
go to exhibitions and concerts. These are not small
audiences, though it would hardly matter if they were.
What objection could there be in principle to forms of
design that treat these audiences as visually aware
and offer them graphic messages as sophisticated as
the cultural forms the messages promote? Perhaps
this work has implications for other areas of graphic
design. Perhaps it can function as a kind of "research
and development". I believe it often does. But even
if most of it proved to have no wider application,
this would not negate its effectiveness for its intended
audience, or detract from its interest as a form of
cultural expression.

    Much the same arguments can be applied to
the even more contentious area of "design about
design", the self-referential promotional projects and
student exercises for which the primary audience will
inevitably be other designers. *The Graphic Edge*, like

How can I show you devotion?
Type study
Designer: Martin J. Venezky
Cranbrook Academy of Art
USA, 1992

Silence
Poster
Designer: David Shields
Cranbrook Academy of Art
USA, 1992

Keep Him Away with the Left Jab!
Poster
Designer/illustrator: Elliott Peter Earls
Cranbrook Academy of Art
USA, 1991

Typography Now, includes a number of examples of this kind of work, from established professionals and students at Yale University and Cranbrook Academy of Art in the US and the Royal College of Art in London. This is not because the ideas contained within these designs can necessarily be translated directly into corporate identities and annual reports – this is far too limiting as a criterion for validity – but because such projects offer valuable safety zones in which designers can legitimately push at the boundaries of the discipline, and because the ideas (generally in a more diffuse form) may eventually come to nourish their commercial work and that of other professionals.

What this collection points up is that even at the experimental end of graphic design there are now two divergent currents: broadly speaking, the complex and the clean. Among the reactions to the kind of work collected in *Typography Now* were those who felt we had reached a point of maximum typographic density and distortion which left only one place to go: back to simplicity. "The limits may have been stretched so far that reevaluation is the logical next move," the critic Steven Heller wrote in an editorial in the *American Institute of Graphic Arts Journal* (vol. 10 no. 1, 1992).

In an issue of *Emigre* – the house magazine of experimental typographers – titled "Starting from Zero" (no. 19, 1991), Rudy VanderLans posed much the same question. Pointing to celebrated renunciations of complexity, from Jan Tschichold's classical conversion to Neville Brody's personal rediscovery of Helvetica, he asked: "Does all experimentation in graphic design lead to the simplification of graphic design? Are the graphic designers who concern themselves with complex solutions merely slow learners who try out the wildest schemes only to come to one conclusion, that less is more?"

Heller was inclined to doubt that simplicity was making a comeback, while the community of international type iconoclasts represented by *Emigre* shows no sign to date of experiencing a crisis of conscience and switching to centred type. And yet, as this book seeks to show, throughout the period in which the more flamboyant experimentalists gained so much publicity, there have been other equally committed attempts to make a contemporary design less reliant on sensational surface effect and more closely wedded to content. Of central importance here, but still little seen or discussed by graphic designers,

The Medium is the Massage
Book spreads
Designer: Quentin Fiore
Random House
USA, 1967

Ways of Seeing
Book cover
Designer: Richard Hollis
Penguin Books
Great Britain, 1972

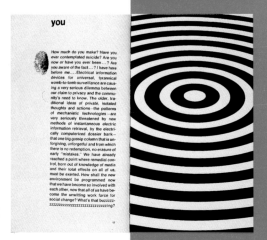

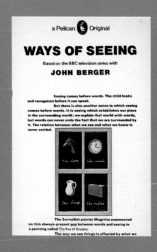

10 11

are two catalogues designed by Dan Friedman for the Deste Foundation for Contemporary Art in Athens.

Friedman, once identified with the post-modern American New Wave, is now a "Radical Modernist" who believes it is the narrow mannerisms of corporate modernism which are ethically and aesthetically bankrupt, not the transforming social and cultural vision of the movement itself. His designs for the catalogues *Artificial Nature* (1990) and *Post Human* (1992) belong to a small but visionary group of publications created since the 1960s which have sought to question and extend the word-dependent format of the printed book. The catalogues' most obvious precursors are the *Commentaires* of Chris Marker (1961 and 1967), collections of his film scripts; the designs of Quentin Fiore, in particular for the Marshall McLuhan reader, *The Medium is the Massage* (1967) – see *Eye* no. 8 vol. 2, 1993; and Richard Hollis' designs for John Berger's *Ways of Seeing* (1972) and Colin MacCabe's *Godard: images, sounds, politics.* (1980). In these books, the stream of picture material does not merely illustrate the words, but becomes an active force in the development of the argument, flowing into the text and out again and

sometimes carrying key ideas without any need of literary reinforcement.

Artificial Nature and *Post Human* work in broadly similar ways. A central essay, written by the exhibitions' curator, Jeffrey Deitch, is bracketed, front and back, by full-page pictures showing work by the artists together with brilliantly researched sequences of lurid photolibrary images germane to the shows' themes. In *Artificial Nature*, the reader is given three ways of accessing Deitch's deadpan argument that nature as a pure, untampered with, elemental phenomenon no longer exists; that we now inhabit an artificially constructed, "post-natural" world of bio-technology, beauty treatments, open-heart surgery, scented air-fresheners and virtual reality headsets. It is possible to read the large-print essay straight through as an ordinary linear text; to scan the keywords highlighted in black bars and key phrases picked out in red brush script; or to browse through the pictures, which are captioned with provocative words or slogan-like phrases drawn from the main essay: "Genuine nature may now be more artificial than natural", "Could it happen that the next generation will be our last generation of real humans?"

Artificial Nature
Exhibition poster (reverse side)
Designer: Dan Friedman
Client: Deste Foundation
for Contemporary Art, Athens
USA, 1990

Love for Sale
Book cover
Designer: Barbara Kruger
Abrams
USA, 1990

Knock. Knock.
Postcard
Designer: Donald Moffett
Co-production by Donald Moffett and
Jersey City Museum
USA, 1992

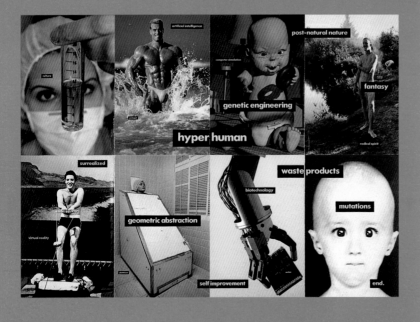

What makes these catalogues so fresh to eyes jaded
by a surfeit of unnecessary styling is that they use
only as much "design" as they need. It is not that they
look undesigned – both books have a strong image
and presence as objects. But this is precisely because
Friedman has the confidence to allow the revelatory
picture material to speak for itself. The simple Futura
captions in *Artificial Nature* are fast-reading conductors
for the catalogues' bolts of humour and satirical
shocks; the pared-down graphic language is well suited
to situations where the editorial message must be
communicated with some urgency. It is an approach
already familiar from the politically motivated, gender-
based work of American artist Barbara Kruger.
Indeed Kruger's career – she started as a magazine
designer and picture editor at Condé Nast – underlines
the complex chain of influence operating in this area,
as the graphic strategies she learned as a professional
designer and applied with such force as a media artist
feed back into graphic design and become part of
its vernacular. The Kruger format – a single telling
word or phrase stamped across an image – can now
be seen everywhere, from the activist graphics
and commercial design projects of Donald Moffett and
Marlene McCarty, alias Bureau, in New York, to the
record sleeve designs of Mark Farrow and HIV/AIDS
awareness cards of Alan Aboud and Sandro
Sodano in London.

For designers working at the cutting edge of
graphic design, the contemporary art scene remains
one of the most valuable testbeds for new ideas.
And it is hardly surprising that art based on an
examination of photographic, printed and televisual
media should in turn prove so seductive and
suggestive for designers. In the 1960s, Pop Art's
transformation of printed sources from commercial
art and popular culture triggered a wave of pop
graphics. In the 1990s, in much the same way, the
new graphic design throws out echoes of artists such
as Edward Ruscha, Lawrence Weiner, John Baldessari
and Richard Prince. The Dutch design duo Armand
Mevis and Linda van Deursen, the English company
Cartlidge Levene, and Elliott Peter Earls, a
postgraduate student at the Cranbrook Academy of
Art, create designs whose structural geometry
and strange dislocated moods show many points
of similarity with art of this kind. Peter Saville
re-appropriates the Marlboro Man advertising icon,

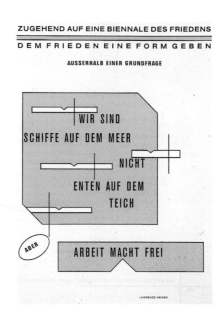

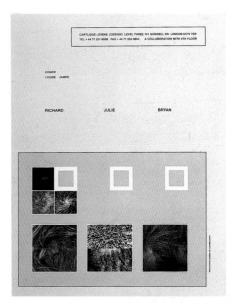

first appropriated by Richard Prince, for the English rock group New Order and designs a series of gloomy press ads for the fashion designer Yohji Yamamoto whose startling disjunctions between client and image were inspired by the art magazine advertising of the Bruno Bischofberger Gallery in Zurich. The gallery used banal Swiss scenes of a rifle range, pig slaughtering and traditional embroidery to represent artists like Andy Warhol and Francesco Clemente. Saville captures the anti-fashion mood of late 1991 with a drooping flower, a downbeat factory scene and a melting hot rod.

Such strategies assume a high degree of visual literacy on the part of the viewer. These particular designs are not visually complex, but they are conceptually subtle. It is not necessary to identify the references to understand this work; it is necessary to accept a more tangential approach to communication than graphic design orthodoxy has traditionally allowed. It is a recurrent criticism of contemporary graphics that it contains too much "self-expression", that designers are putting their own creative interests before the needs of their clients, and that the client's message is being muddled, misunderstood or lost in

the process. The trouble with these criticisms is that they indiscriminately lump the good with the bad, as though one feeble play, or a thousand feeble plays, made every play feeble. This is because they start from an untenable premise – that absolute, selfless neutrality is both desirable and possible for all kinds of graphic design – which leaves no room for manoeuvre. Real examples are rarely named or discussed, making it hard to respond to these assertions, nor is "self-expression", in this implicitly pejorative sense, defined with any precision. It is hard to imagine what a poster, book, calendar, or brochure design entirely devoid of "self" would be like, unless it was generated entirely by machine, so presumably the real issue (notwithstanding the rhetoric) is a matter of degree. There comes a point for these critics, whatever the context, at which there is just too much subjective self and not enough objective message in a design. At this point they cry "art".

The problem, I believe, lies in the way we define our terms. We take two categories, "art" and "design", define them as two quite different processes (despite the fact that they clearly have a great deal in common) and insist that visual communication falls

Regret
by New Order
Record sleeve
Art director: Peter Saville
Designer: Brett Wickens
Design company: Pentagram
Photographer: photolibrary
Client: CentreDate/London Records
Great Britain, 1993

Hover Hover
Billboard
Designers: Armand Mevis, Linda van Deursen
Design company: Mevis & van Deursen
Client: Stedelijk Museum, Amsterdam
The Netherlands, 1991

neatly into one category or the other, with no blurring or overlap allowed. It is not clear why we feel that the integrity of these categories has to be defended so dogmatically, except that designers have a vested professional interest in design, the art world has a similar interest in preserving the untouchability of art, and the education of designers and artists, by splitting the two groups, tends to reflect and reinforce these polarities. Historically, of course, before the two fields became so thoroughly professionalised the distinctions were less rigidly drawn. There are plenty of twentieth-century examples of individuals who have operated effectively in both camps without troubling about their job descriptions, but a historical digression is not necessary here. My point is rather more pragmatic and rooted in the present: whether the more conservative critics of the profession like it or not, there is now a large body of "design", including many of the examples in this book, which implicitly, by its very existence, challenges these definitions. Denouncing it will not make it go away or solve the problem. So why not accept that the communication arts are evolving, that there is good work in this area as well as mediocre and derivative work (as in any other branch

of design), and enlarge our restricting and no longer viable definitions instead?

The situation is if anything about to become even more complex. Graphic designers have not been especially quick to grasp the implications of digital multimedia, and the earliest examples of the genre have badly lacked their imaginative input. This will slowly change as designers come to terms with the technology in their own studios and begin to think beyond the paper applications of the tools. Multimedia by its very nature is about the collapse of traditional boundaries and the flowing together of categories into new forms of communication, about which we can as yet only speculate. The designers likely to make the biggest impact in this area will be those who can cope with the challenge of conceptual uncertainty.

If Dan Friedman's work represents one pole of the new graphic design, then Cranbrook Academy of Art graduate P. Scott Makela stands at the other. Friedman has expressed doubts about the divisive effects of digital culture. While his designs imply many of the structural and associational freedoms of multimedia, they do not suggest some new, differently textured form of information experience; they belong

Redefining Display
Project for *Design Quarterly*
Magazine cover (front and back)
Designer: P. Scott Makela with Alex Tylevich
Magazine designer: Laurie Haycock Makela
Client: Walker Art Center, Minneapolis
USA, Winter 1993

to the 500-year tradition of the printed book. Makela, a self-styled cyberpunk who uses the boast "100% digital" as his calling card, is leaving paper behind. He is equally at home with the technologies of design, music and video and is increasingly merging all three. Scanning one of his clotted and centreless digital designs is like floating across an electronic firestorm, wondering where it would be safe to touch down. The effect, he notes, is entirely deliberate. "When I see a lot of white space in a design, and when something is really 'arranged', the design becomes contained by the borders . . . like pieces on a plate. I have a need to move off the plate. What I am trying to do is grab a chunk of experience and have that bleed off all edges" (*Emigre* no. 23, 1992). Printed projects such as Makela's prospectus for The Minneapolis College of Art and Design and visual essay for the publication *Rethinking Design* are perhaps best interpreted as two-dimensional electronic paintings of multimedia environments for which we do not yet have the technology. Stunning as they are, it is debatable whether or not they fully succeed as paper-bound communication simply because – as with other digital designs of this complexity – the frozen page and its

static frame work against images that feel as though their natural condition is fluid, reactive and temporal.

Makela himself seems to acknowledge the transitional nature of such designs. In a remarkable speculative project for the journal *Design Quarterly* (no. 158, Winter 1993), modelled on his own studio experiences of switching between software programs, E-mail, electronic bulletin boards, CD player and satellite TV, he visualises the electronic office screens of a priest, a plumber, a motorcycle mechanic and a multimedia artist. The priest listens to a man in a teleconfessional and sifts through religious texts, while the plumber files invoices, deals with an angry client and dreams of a fishing trip. Each of these fictional characters can arrange the on-screen electronic information exactly as they would the papers, gadgets and personal belongings on a desk. For anyone who is sceptical about the aesthetic possibilities of multimedia, given the rather meagre evidence so far, Makela's project will have resonance. Here, with a detail and conviction few other graphic designers working in this field have achieved, we see a glimpse of what the dawning fusion of art, design and technology may hold.

Rick Poynor

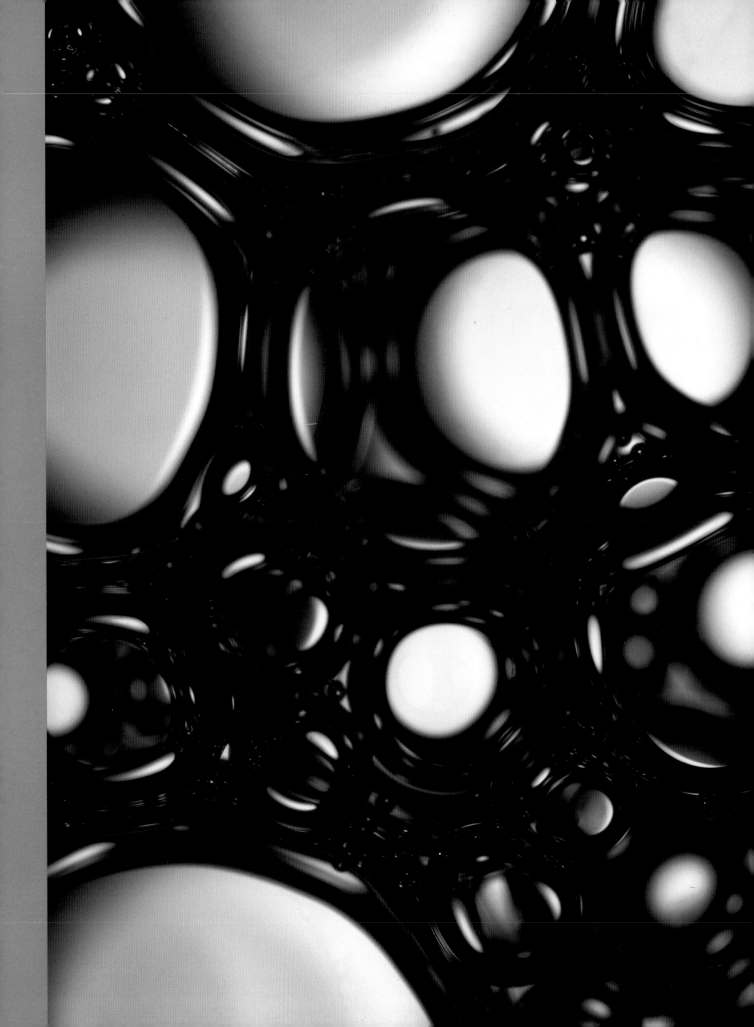

cool

L'Invitation au Voyage
Book cover
Designer: Allen Hori
Design company: Hard Werken Design
Client: Rijksdienst Beeldende Kunst,
The Hague
The Netherlands, 1991

Adopt a Book
Poster
Designer: Lucille Tenazas
Design company: Tenazas Design
Photographer: Peter de Lory
Client: California College of Arts and Crafts
USA, 1992

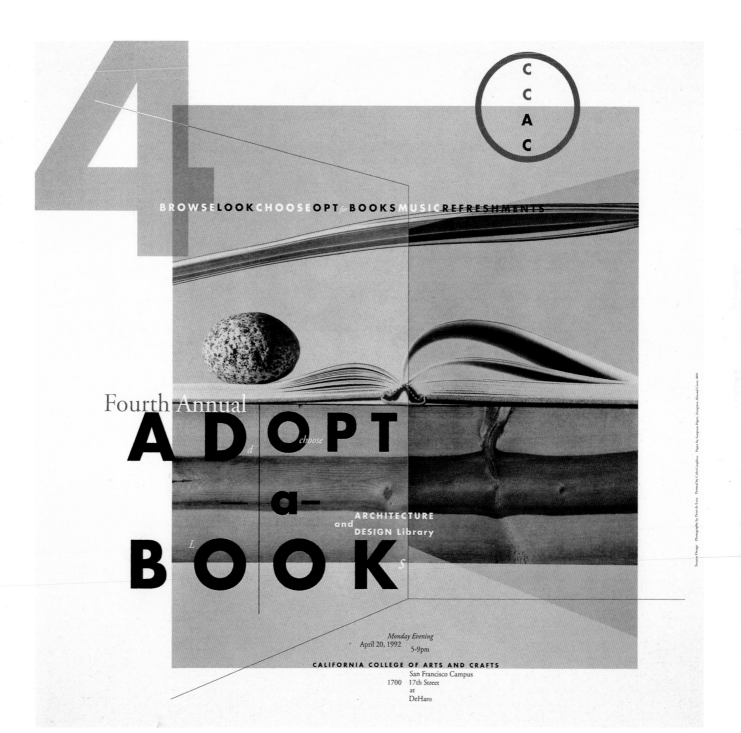

Tactics of Posture
Poster
Designer: Andrew Blauvelt
Client: Washington University Gallery of Art
USA, 1991

Anatomy Calendar 93
April
Designer: Vaughan Oliver
Design company: v23
Photographer: Jim Friedman
Client: 4AD
Great Britain, 1992

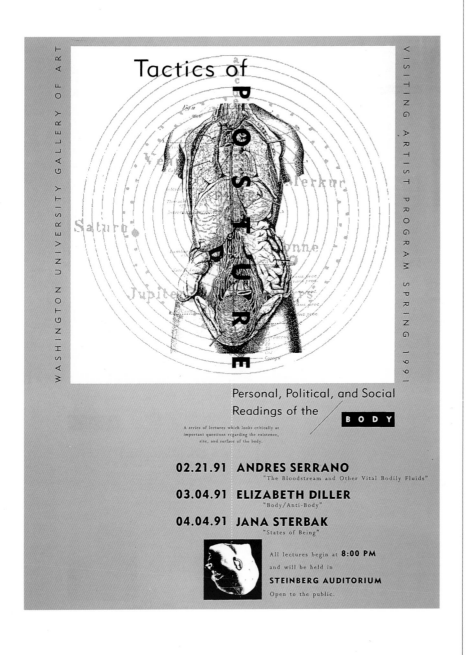

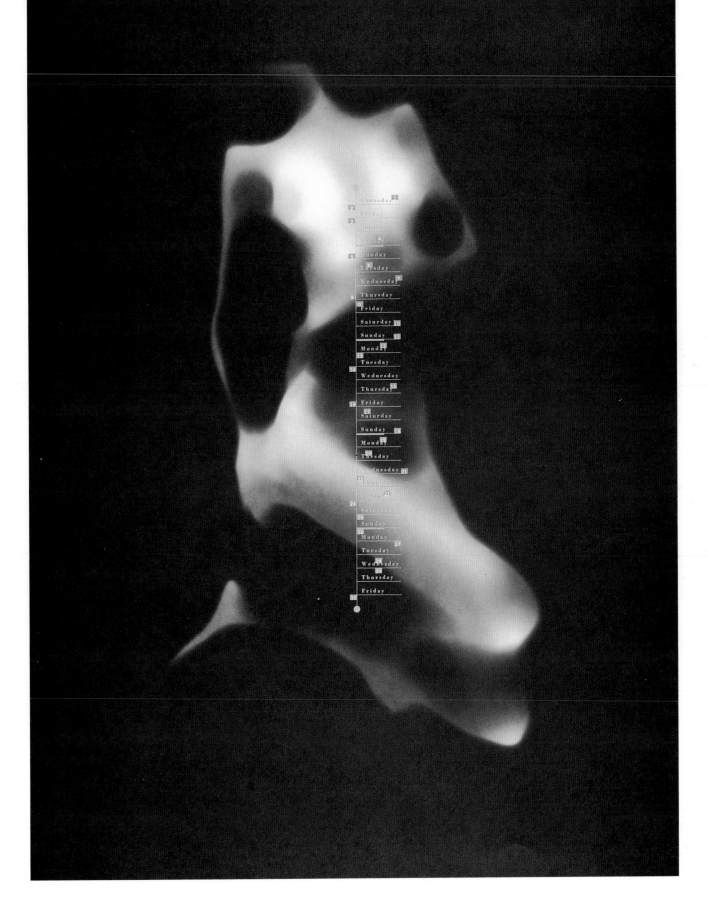

Systems Manual
Brochure for hi-fi consultant
Designer: Paul Elliman
Photographer: Moira Bogue
Client: The Cornflake Shop
Great Britain, 1991

Multi-room
Advertisement for hi-fi consultant
Designer: Paul Elliman
Photographer: Moira Bogue
Client: The Cornflake Shop
Great Britain, 1991

Cobalt Blue
Album cover
Designers: Vaughan Oliver, Chris Bigg
Design company: v23
Illustrator: Russell Mills
Photographer: Simon Larbalestier
Modelmaker: Pirate
Client: 4AD
Great Britain, 1992

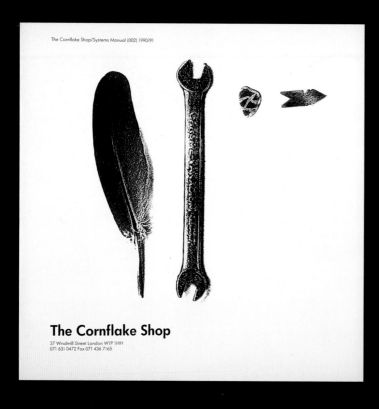

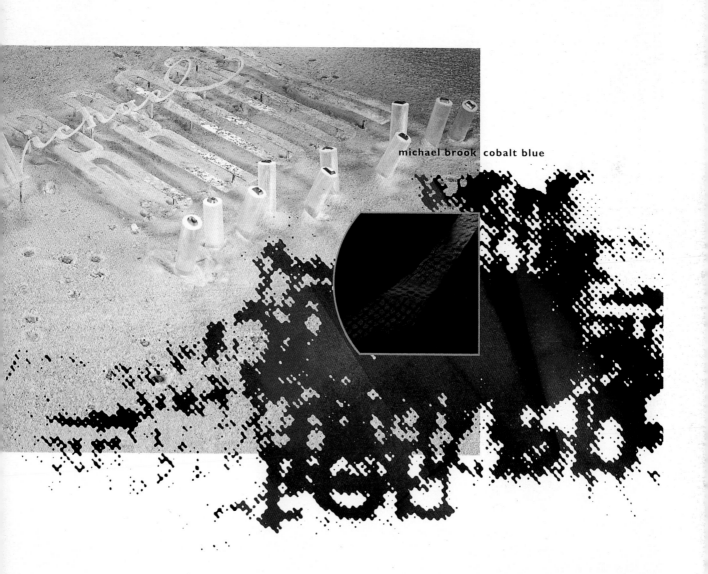

michael brook cobalt blue

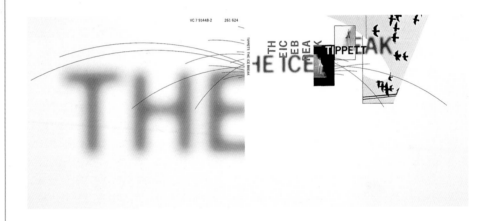

VC 7 91448-2   261 624

TIPPETT, THE ICE BREAK

type

gners: a biographical directory

type designers:

by Ron Eason & Sarah Rookledge, edited by Phil Baines & Gordon Rookledge

'...its extensive list of type designers, punch-cutters and foundries makes it unique.'

Hans Arnold, Senior Designer, Wolff Olins

Over a period of thirty years **Ron Eason** has worked on the production of books and periodicals with leading British printers, including The Westerham Press and the former Gavin Martin Ltd. Married with two children, he lives in the Surrey countryside. Born in 1962, **Sarah Rookledge** graduating from Warwick University where she studied film and literature after working for Salisbury Publishing Services Ltd, she entered book publishing with a move to Sarema Press (Publishers) Ltd. She now works as a short-story writer and freelance journalist and lives in London. **Phil Baines** (born 1958), has worked as a freelance graphic designer since graduating from the Royal College of Art in 1987, combining this with teaching part-time at Central Saint Martin's College of Art & Design in London. **Gordon Rookledge**, 57, is the founder (1983), and Managing Director of art and graphic book publishers Sarema Press (Publishers) Ltd. He is on the committee of the Wynken de Worde Society; married with three children he lives in both London and Brighton.

'The Handbook of Type Designers differs from other type books by putting the typefaces into context and providing fascinating information about the people behind the typefaces.'

Jon Barnbrook

As a one-off only pre-publication offer this book is available at a discounted price.

Rookledge's International hand–book of type desi–gners:

offer expires 30-9-91

5

SAREMA PRESS

Designed by Nick Bell. Typeset by The Typeform. Printed in England by DTR 9/93. 1m.

The Ice Break
CD packaging
Designer: Nick Bell
Art director: Jeremy Hall
Photographer: Nick Bell
Client: Virgin Classics
Great Britain, 1991

**Rookledge's International
Handbook of Type Designers**
Leaflet
Designer: Nick Bell
Client: Sarema Press
Great Britain, 1991

Typography as Discourse
Poster (reverse side)
Designers: Andrew Blauvelt, James Sholly,
Laura Lacy-Sholly
Photographer: Andrew Blauvelt
Client: Art Directors Club of Indiana
USA, 1991

Herron's educational program provides the student with a series of studio art experiences balanced by classes in the humanities and sciences. Through this educational program, Herron is able to produce artists and designers who are truly **visual professionals,** able to contribute to their chosen professions and society at large.

Students at the Herron School of Art are surrounded by the vibrancy and intensity of a visual arts environment. The School's 400 students work closely with the full-time faculty, with a student teacher ratio of approximately 11:1. This small class size allows students to obtain the close personal attention necessary for their artistic development. At Herron, the emphasis is on **artists teaching artists.** The faculty are practicing artists, designers, and art educators. Their professional experience reinforces their teaching performance. All Herron courses are taught by faculty members rather than graduate students.

The combination of an excellent faculty, well-designed programs of instruction, and outstanding equipment and facilities provides an ideal educational setting for the preparation of **a career in the visual arts.**

Graduates of the School's programs can be found in professional positions throughout the United States and in various parts of the world.
Many visual artists can be found working independently while others take careers in arts administration with galleries, agencies, and museums. Designers can be found employed in various positions within advertising agencies, design offices, corporations, and not-for-profit institutions. Graduates of the program in art education also are certified to teach art in the public schools of Indiana.

Herron Viewbook
Brochure spreads
Designer: Andrew Blauvelt
Photographer: Andrew Blauvelt
Client: Herron School of Art
USA, 1991

Podriga Pipeline Appeal
Poster
Designer: Nick Bell
Photographers: Robbie Mahoney,
Colin Edwards
Client: Romanian Project (UK)
Great Britain, 1992

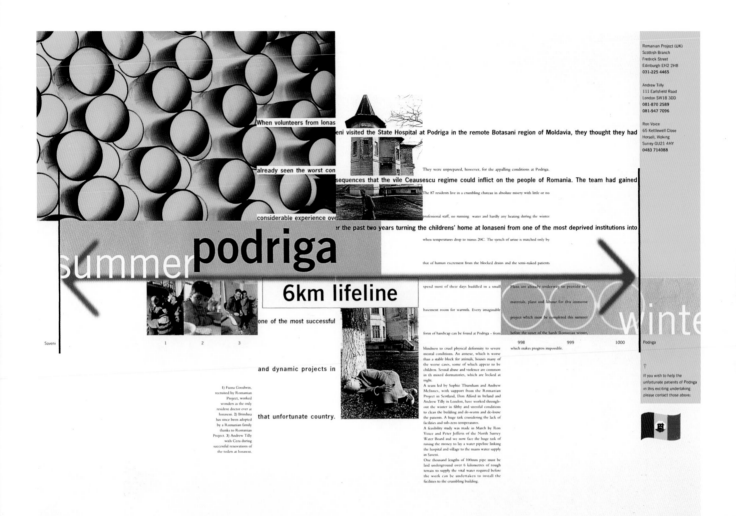

¿CUÁNTO? how much?

$ 100.000.000

Life insurance bought by a major U.S. entertainment corporation for a top executive. How could one person be worth that much money? In show business, where multimillion-dollar deals are made based on nebulous commodities like "box office appeal," an executive's personal contacts and gut instincts are fixed assets, just as an oil tanker or a factory are fixed assets in other businesses.

Seguro de vida ofrecido por una compañía estadounidense a uno de sus máximos ejecutivos. ¿Cómo puede valer tanto una persona? En el mundo del "entertainment", donde se hacen contratos multi-millonarios sobre mercancía tan vaga como la "atracción taquillera", los contactos personales y los instintos de un ejecutivo se convierten en activos fijos tal como un tanque de petróleo o una fábrica lo son en otros negocios.

$ 36.000.000

British newspaper magnate Robert Maxwell's life insurance policy. His body was found floating in the Atlantic Ocean near the Canary Islands, but Lloyd's of London says, "There will be no payout." Shoulder-muscle injuries, according to investigators, indicate that Maxwell may have eased himself over the side of his yacht and held on "for a time with one or both hands before letting go."

Póliza del seguro de vida del magnate británico Robert Maxwell. Su cuerpo fue hallado flotando en el Océano Atlántico cerca de las Islas Canarias, pero según Lloyd's of London, "No va a haber pago". De acuerdo a los investigadores, las lesiones que tenía en los hombros indican que Maxwell se pudo haber colgado de un lado del yate, "por algún tiempo con una o con ambas manos antes de soltarse".

$ 2.600.000

Offered for the death of British author Salman Rushdie after the publication of The Satanic Verses in 1989. This reward, promised by Ayatollah Khomeini, is only for Iranians. In a separate deal, foreigners were promised US$1.000.000 by Iranian cleric Hassan Sanei, who doubled his price to US$2.000.000 in 1991. The novel is now out in paperback.

Oferta por la vida del escritor británico Salman Rushdie hecha después de la publicación de su libro Los Versos Satánicos en 1989. Esta recompensa ofrecida por el Ayatola Jomeini es sólo para iraníes. A los extranjeros, Hassan Sanei, un imán iraní prometió pagar un millón de dólares, precio que subió a dos millones en 1991. La novela ya está disponible en su edición bolsillo.

$ 1.600.000

Demanded by inept Russian kidnappers for an Australian computer-firm executive, Daniel Weinstock, and his wife Yvonne. The couple was rescued through the joint efforts of the American FBI (a relative in the United States was contacted for the ransom money) and the Agency for Federal Security (formerly the KGB).

Recompensa exigida por unos ineptos secuestradores rusos por el rescate del ejecutivo de una compañía de computadoras australiana, Daniel Weinstock y esposa Ivonne. La pareja fue rescatada gracias a un esfuerzo conjunto entre el FBI (pues un familiar en los EE.UU. fue contactado para conseguir el dinero) y la Agencia Federal de Seguridad (antes conocida como la KGB).

$ 350.000

Offered by Colombian drug kingpin Carlos Lehder to anyone who would kill the head of the United States Drug Enforcement Administration, Francis "Bud" Mullin. No one took him up on it. Only US$125.000 was paid for the assassination of Colonel Jaime Ramírez-Gómez, chief of the Colombian anti-narcotics police.

Oferta hecha por el narcotraficante colombiano Carlos Lehder a cualquiera que matara al jefe de la DEA, Francis "Bud" Mullin. Pero nadie se aprovechó. Por el asesinato del coronel Jaime Ramírez Gómez, jefe de la policía anti-narcóticos colombiana, se pagaron US$125.000.

$ 26.000

"Blood money" required for the death of a Muslim man in Saudi Arabia. The fee, paid to the family of a murder or accident victim, allows the perpetrator to go free. US$13.000 is the amount for a non-Muslim man, a Muslim woman or child. Only US$6.500 for non-Muslim women and children.

"Dinero sangriento" o remuneración por matar a un hombre musulmán en Arabia Saudita. La cuota, requerida bajo una ley saudita, se le paga a la familia de la víctima y permite que el acusado mantenga su libertad. La muerte puede o no ser accidental. El precio por un hombre no-musulmán, así como por una mujer o niño musulmán es de US$13.000. Por una mujer o niño no-musulmán el precio es de US$6.500.

$ 15.000

Maximum compensation established by the United Nations for loss of a family member caused by Iraq's invasion of Kuwait, to be funded by Iraqi oil sales. The family of an Egyptian soldier received only US$1.500 from the Egyptian government for his death in the Gulf War. They were thrilled when the soldier returned home alive and they got to keep the money.

Compensación máxima establecida por las Naciones Unidas por la pérdida de un familiar durante la invasión de Irak a Kuwait. El dinero proviene de las ventas de petróleo iraquí. La familia de un soldado egipcio recibió US$1.500 del gobierno egipcio por la muerte de su hijo en la guerra del Golfo Pérsico. Pero la felicidad les sobrevino cuando el hijo regresó sano y salvo y además se quedaron con el dinero.

$ 8.000

Paid to the professional killer of a local politician in Naples, Italy. Most hired killers in Italy are amateurs, often under the age of 18 (they get a reduced sentence) or under 14 (they don't get indicted at all). Rates are roughly US$1.200 for a regular person (in one instance, the custodian of a soccer field) and in Sicily, Calabria, or Campania, a hit can be had for as little as US$240.

Pago a un asesino profesional por matar a un político local en Nápoles, Italia. Casi todos los asesinos son amateurs y menores de 18 años (reciben una sentencia menor) o de 14 años (no reciben sentencia alguna). Los precios varían. Por una persona común y corriente se paga más o menos US$1.200 (como el de un guardián en un campo de fútbol). Mientras en Sicilia, Calabria o Campania se mata hasta por US$240.

$ 4.100

Dowry paid by a 61-year-old Saudi Arabian man to a family in Hyderabad, India for an 11-year-old bride. A stewardess noticed the girl crying on an Air India flight to Saudi Arabia and when the plane stopped in New Delhi, the man was arrested. But Islamic Hyderabad remains a source of discount brides for Saudis who would have to pay higher prices at home.

Dote pagada por un hombre saudita de 61 años a una familia en Haiderabad por una novia de11 años. Una azafata de Aero India notó a la niña llorando en un vuelo que iba a Arabia Saudita. Y cuando el avión hizo escala en Nueva Delhi arrestaron al hombre. Pero en Haiderabad islámico sigue siendo más barato para las saudíes obtener esposas que en su propia tierra.

$ 230

Price paid for a Filipino university student who was kidnapped and held as one of 32 sex slaves on a marijuana plantation for almost four years before she escaped. No ransom was demanded. "This is a case of white slavery," commented Dipilog police chief Aquilino Garate.

Precio que se pagó por secuestrar a una estudiante filipina que luego fue usada como una de las 32 esclavas sexuales en una plantación de marijuana de la que escapó cuatro años después. Nunca se pidió rescate. "Esto fue un caso de trata de blancas", comentó el jefe de la policía de Dipilog, Aquilino Garate.

$ 100

Plus an unknown quantity of marijuana, was what a 23-year-old Georgia, USA man, Jeffery Roberts, was paid by Debra Thomas, 33, to strangle her common-law husband. The prosecution produced letters exchanged by Roberts and Thomas in jail as proof that the motive was desire. "I have a constant aching for you," Thomas wrote to Roberts.

Fue lo que recibió Jeffery Roberts, de 23 años, de Debra Thomas, de 33, por estrangular a su marido, mas cantidad desconocida de marijuana. La fiscalía presentó las cartas que se escribieron Roberts y Thomas en la cárcel como prueba de que fue un crimen pasional. "Tengo unas ganas insaciables de ti", Thomas le escribió a Roberts.

$ 0,11

Cost of a bullet in China. More than 40 crimes in that country are punishable by death, including printing pornography and bribing the police. In the 1980s, after an execution by firing squad, the family of the executed was sometimes required to pay for the bullet.

Costo de una bala en la China. En los años ochenta, después de una ejecución, la familia del ejecutado algunas veces tenía que pagar por la bala, incluyendo la publicación de material pornográfico y el soborno a policías. En China más de 40 crímenes conllevan la pena de muerte.

$ 40 — Price per kilo paid by East Asian and European wig makers for Indian HAIR longer than 30 centimeters. Shorter hair fetches half the price and scraps from the barbershop floor, bought by chemical companies, go for US$2 a kilo. The Lord Venkateswara Temple in Tirupati, India, earns about US$500.000 annually by selling hair shaved from the heads of pilgrims.

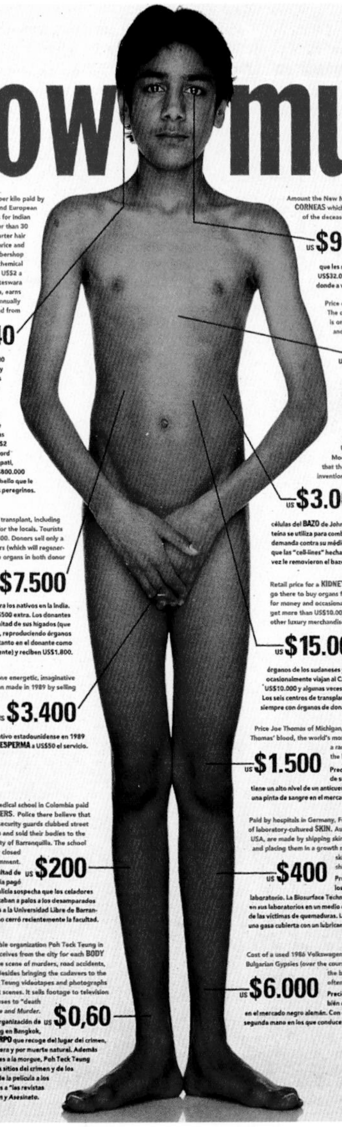

Precio por kilo que pagan los fabricantes de pelucas de Asia del Este y de Europa por CABELLO indio de más de 30 centímetros de largo muy cotizado por los asiáticos y los europeos que hacen pelucas. El cabello corto se vende por mitad de precio y los sobrantes en los suelos de las peluquerías, los compran las compañías químicas, se venden por US$2 el kilo. El templo de Lord Venkateswara en Tirupati, India, gana cerca de US$500.000 anuales por vender el cabello que le rasuran a los peregrinos.

$ 3.400 — What one energetic, imaginative American man made in 1989 by selling his SPERM at US$50 a pop.

Fue lo que ganó un energético e imaginativo estadounidense en 1989 vendiendo su ESPERMA a US$50 el servicio.

$ 200 — Amount a medical school in Colombia paid for CADAVERS. Police there believe that university security guards clubbed street people to death and sold their bodies to the Free University of Barranquilla. The school was recently closed by the government.

Monto que una facultad de medicina en Colombia pagó por CADÁVERES. La policía sospecha que los celadores de la universidad mataban a palos a los desamparados y vendían sus cuerpos a la Universidad Libre de Barranquilla. El gobierno cerró recientemente la facultad.

$ 0,60 — What the charitable organization Poh Teck Teung in Bangkok, Thailand, receives from the city for each BODY it collects from the scene of murders, road accidents, and natural deaths. Besides bringing the cadavers to the morgue, Poh Teck Teung videotapes and photographs crime and accident scenes. It sells footage to television news and photos of corpses to "death magazines" like Crime and Murder.

Es lo que recibe la organización de caridad Poh Teck Teung en Bangkok, Tailandia, por cada CUERPO que recoja del lugar del crimen, de accidentes en la carretera y por muerte natural. Además de llevar los cadáveres a la morgue, Poh Teck Teung filma y fotografía los sitios del crimen y de los accidentes. Luego vende la película a los noticieros y las fotografías a "las revistas de muerte" como Crimen y Asesinato.

$ 900 — Amount the New Mexico, USA, Lions Eye Bank charges hospitals for CORNEAS which are removed from corpses with the authorization of the deceased's family. US$32.000 is the black market price for corneas in Argentina where the entire lens of the eye is sometimes removed without permission.

Cifra por US$32.000 es el precio en el mercado negro de corneas en Argentina, donde a veces se remueve la lente completa del ojo sin permiso. Indio de más de 30 centímetros, EE.UU., cobra a los hospitales por las CORNEAS que les sacan a los cadáveres con autorización de la familia del muerto.

$ 91.000 — Price of a secondhand HEART, fully installed, in the USA. The cost of acquiring the organ (including shipping and handling) is only US$12.578, while the hospital charges over US$62.000 and the surgeon's fee comes to US$10.000. For an additional US$43.000 they'll throw

Precio de un CORAZÓN de segunda mano, totalmente instalado. El costo del órgano (incluyendo los costos de correo) es sólo de US$12.578, mientras el hospital cobra más de US$62.000 y la cuota del cirujano alcanza los US$10.000. Por US$43.000 adicionales incluyen un par de pulmones.

$ 3.000.000.000 — Alleged market value of a protein made of cells from a SPLEEN which was surgically removed from John Moore of California, USA. The protein is used to combat immune-system deficiencies. Moore took his doctor for a share of the profits, but judges ruled that the "cell-lines" made from Moore's tissue were a "product of invention" and that once the spleen was removed from his body, Moore no longer had any claim to it.

Supuesto valor de una proteína hecha con las células del BAZO de John Moore de California, que le fue removido en una clínica. La proteína se utiliza para combatir las deficiencias del sistema inmunológico. Moore entabló una demanda contra su médico para que compartiera las ganancias, pero los jueces decidieron que las "cell-lines" hechas del tejido de Moore eran un "producto de invención" y que una vez le removieron el bazo él no tenía ningún derecho sobre el órgano.

$ 15.000 — Retail price for a KIDNEY in Cairo, Egypt. Wealthy Persian Gulf Arabs go there to buy organs from penniless Sudanese and Somalis who are desperate for money and occasionally travel to Cairo specifically to sell a kidney. Donors can get more than US$10.000 and are sometimes offered apartments, televisions, and other luxury merchandise. Cairo's six kidney transplant centers perform roughly 350 operations a year, always taking the organs from live donors.

Valor de un RIÑON al menudeo en el Cairo, Egipto. Árabes ricachones del Golfo Pérsico van a comprar órganos de los sudaneses y somalíes pobretones que desesperados por conseguir dinero ocasionalmente viajan al Cairo para vender sus riñones. Los donantes reciben más de US$10.000 y algunas veces les ofrecen apartamentos, televisores y otros artículos de lujo. Los seis centros de transplantes del Cairo llevan a cabo cerca de 350 operaciones al año siempre con órganos de donantes vivos.

$ 1.500 — Price Joe Thomas of Michigan, USA, gets for a quart (about a liter) of his BLOOD. Thomas' blood, the world's most valuable, has the highest known level of Anti-Lewis B, a rare antibody. The street value of a half liter of blood on the black market in Nigeria is US$8.

Precio que recibe Joe Thomas de Michigan, EE.UU., por un cuarto de su SANGRE. La sangre de Thomas, la más valiosa del mundo, tiene un alto nivel de un anticuerpo raro conocido como Anti-Lewis B. El valor en la calle de una pinta de sangre en el mercado negro de Nigeria es US$8.

$ 400 — Paid by hospitals in Germany, France, Argentina, and the USA for 25 square centimeters of laboratory-cultured SKIN. Autografts, sold by BioSurface Technology of Massachusetts, USA, are made by shipping skin cells from hospitalized burn victims to the company lab and placing them in a growth medium made of nutrients. The cells grow into pieces of skin which are mounted on lubricant-covered gauze and shipped by air freight back to the patient.

Precio pagado por hospitales en Alemania, Francia, Argentina y los EE.UU. por 25 centímetros cuadrados de PIEL cultivada en un laboratorio. La Biosurface Technology de Massachusetts, EE.UU., vende auto-injertos hechos en sus laboratorios en un medio hecho de nutrientes. Las células se convierten en pedazos de piel que se empacan en una gasa cubierta con un lubricante y se envían por correo aéreo de vuelta a los pacientes.

$ 6.000 — Cost of a used 1986 Volkswagen Golf with two doors. This is also the price paid to Bulgarian Gypsies (over the course of three visits) who sell their BONE MARROW on the black market in Germany. With that earnings, the Gypsies often purchase secondhand Western cars and drive them home.

Precio de un Volkswagen Golf 1986, de dos puertas, usado. Es también el precio pagado a los gitanos búlgaros por su MEDULA OSEA. Con estas ganancias los gitanos suelen comprar carros europeos de segunda mano en los que conducen de vuelta a su país.

Colors, issue 3
Magazine spread
Designers: Tibor Kalman, Paul Ritter
Design company: M&Co
Photographer: Oliviero Toscani
Client: Benetton
USA, Fall/Winter 1992

Colors, issue 2
Magazine spread
Designers: Tibor Kalman, Gary Koepke
Design company: M&Co
Client: Benetton
USA, Spring/Summer 1992

We have a lot in common: two ears, two eyes, a silly nose and roughly twenty square feet (and seven pounds) of skin...

SO, what's the difference?

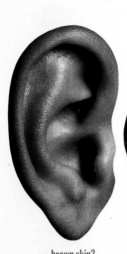

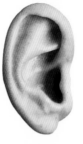

brown skin?
la pelle marrone?

black skin?
la pelle nera?

white skin?
la pelle bianca?

Abbiamo parecchio in comune: due orecchi, due occhi, un naso buffo e circa due metri quadri (e tre chili) di pelle...

e allora, qual'è la differenza?

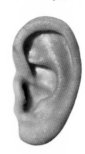

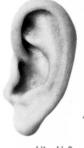

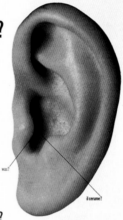

orange skin?
la pelle arancione?

very white skin?
la pelle bianchissima?

asian skin?
la pelle orientale?

So, what's the difference? It depends on who you are and where you live.

E allora? Qual'è la differenza? Dipende da chi sei e da dove vivi.

Colors, issue 4, "Race"
Magazine spreads
Designers: Tibor Kalman, Paul Ritter
Design company: M&Co
Photographer: Oliviero Toscani
Retouchers: Site One
Client: Benetton
USA, Spring/Summer 1993

what if..?

e se..?

We've told you

about skin color, **wax**
ear consistency
and **nose** size. Now,
what do you **really**
want to know about

Ti
abbiamo parlato

del colore della **pelle**, della consistenza del
cerume e delle **naso**. Ma cosa vorresti
sapere **davvero** sulle razze diverse dalla tua **?**

people of other races? Ne eravamo sicuri.

Power

LCO*10*

London
Chamber
Orchestra
Tchaikovsky
Vivaldi
Albinoni
Mozart
Glass
Britten
Bicât
Elgar

LCO 10: Power
Album cover
Designer: Mike Dempsey
Design company: Carroll, Dempsey & Thirkell
Photographer: Lewis Mulatero
Great Britain, 1990

Figaro's Wedding
Theatre poster
Designer: Mike Dempsey
Design company: Carroll, Dempsey & Thirkell
Photographer: Lewis Mulatero
Great Britain, 1992

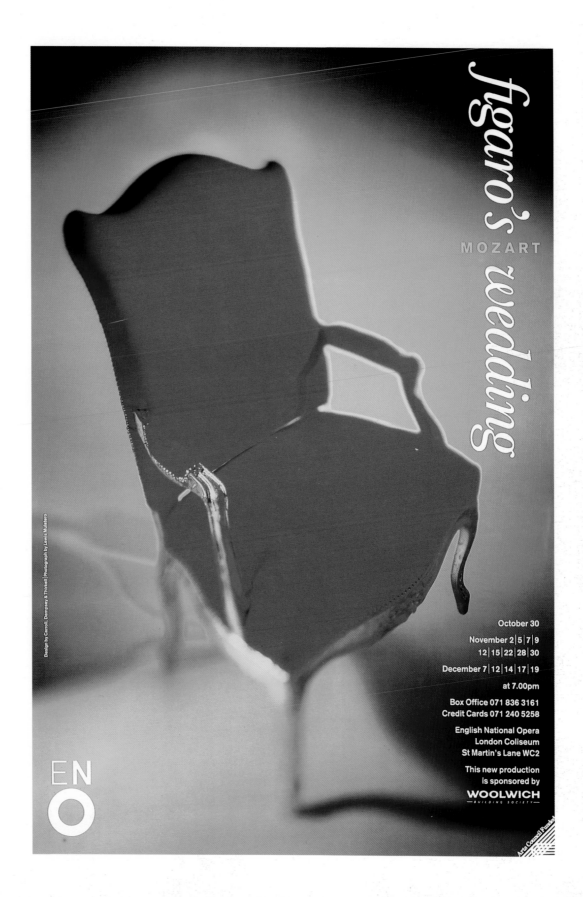

figaro's
MOZART
wedding

October 30
November 2|5|7|9
12|15|22|28|30
December 7|12|14|17|19

at 7.00pm

Box Office 071 836 3161
Credit Cards 071 240 5258

English National Opera
London Coliseum
St Martin's Lane WC2

This new production
is sponsored by
WOOLWICH
BUILDING SOCIETY

EN
O

Design by Carroll, Dempsey & Thirkell | Photograph by Lewis Mulatero

Arts Council Funded

No Limit/Free your Mind
Poster
Designer: Tom Bonauro
Photographer: Jeffery Newbury
Client: Frameline
USA, 1989

Like nothing else in Tennessee
Exhibition poster
Designers: A. Arefin, Stephen Coates
Design company: Arefin Coates
Photographer: A. Arefin
Client: Serpentine Gallery, London
Great Britain, 1992

17 MARCH – 26 APRIL 1992

like nothing

else

in tennessee

REFERENCES TO ARCHITECTURE IN RECENT SCULPTURE, INSTALLATION & PHOTOGRAPHY

jürgen albrecht
siah armajani
ludger gerdes
marin kasimir
hubert kiecol
langlands and bell
matt mullican
maria nordman
julian opie
thomas schütte
dan graham
special commission for the Serpentine Gallery lawn
made possible by the Lisson Gallery

exhibition catalogue sponsored by the
Academy Group Limited

serpentine gallery

Admission free Open daily 10am - 6pm
Talks about the exhibition every Sunday at 3pm
Underground: Lancaster Gate / South Kensington
Buses: 9 10 12 52

Kensington Gardens
London W2 3XA
Telephone 071 402 6075

METAPHORICAL

TOPICAL

PHYSICAL

THEORETICAL

LUBRICATED

UNCOMPLICATED

**INSTITUTE OF CONTEMPORARY ARTS
THE MALL, LONDON** SW1 TEL·071 930 0493

Press advertisement
Designer: A. Arefin
Photographer: Richard J. Burbridge
Client: Institute of Contemporary Arts,
London
Great Britain, 1992

Halluçienda
Club poster
Designers: Peter Saville, Julian Morey
Design company: Peter Saville Associates
Photographer: Anthony Burgess,
Science Photo Library
Client: Fac 51
Great Britain, 1989

lux

Europæ

Edinburgh

Outdoor light
installations by over
forty European
artists across the
City of Edinburgh,
Scotland

For further information   fax: +44 31 557 2500

Principal funders:
Edinburgh District Council
Lothian Regional Council
Lothian and Edinburgh Enterprise Limited
European Arts Festival Fund
Scottish Arts Council
The Henry Moore Foundation
Commission of the European Communities,
Kaleidoscope Fund
Foreign & Commonwealth Office
Visiting Arts

Lux Europæ
Advertisement for exhibition
Designers: A. Arefin, Stephen Coates
Design company: Arefin Coates
Photographers: Nitin Vadukul,
Heidi Kosanuik
Client: Lux Europæ, Edinburgh
Great Britain, 1992

The Winter's Tale
Theatre programme
Designer: Russell Warren-Fisher
Photographer: Gareth McCarthy
Client: Theatre de Complicite
Great Britain, 1991

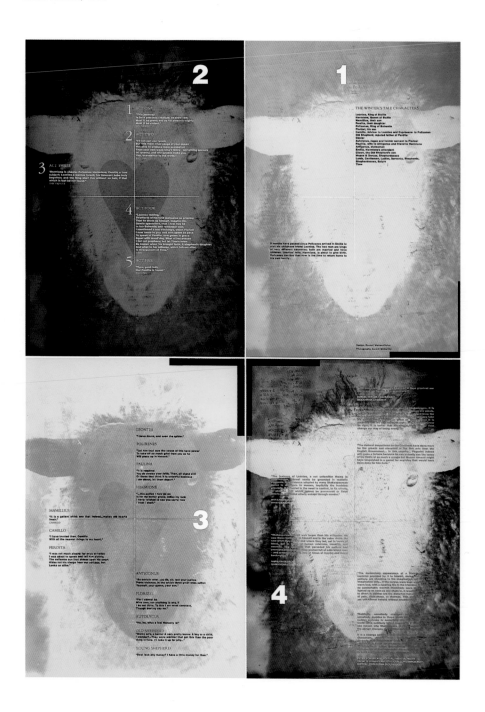

Call for Vision
Poster announcing San Francisco
waterfront competition (reverse side)
Designers: Lucille Tenazas, Todd Foreman
Design company: Tenazas Design
Photographer: Simon Yuen
Client: Center for Critical Architecture
USA, 1992

De Stad
(The City)
Architectural poster
Designers: Ben Faydherbe, Wout de Vringer
Design company: Faydherbe/De Vringer
Client: CBK-Artoteek, Dordrecht
The Netherlands, 1991

EXTRA

Herz, Korte Kalkhaven 1, Dordrecht

de stad

20 11 1991

De stad is een werkgroep
met als doel het verbeteren
van de kwaliteit van de
architectuur en de openbare
ruimte in Dordrecht

Op woensdag 20 november organiseert De Stad
op verzoek van de Dienst Stadsontwikkeling een
discussieavond over:

Drie ontwerpen voor het Statenplein

VROOM & DREESMANN

Michiel Cohen, Van Plesman: Partner

Gunnar Daan: Gunnar Daan Architektuur

Vincent Reijers: Reijers Architekten

De discussie staat onder leiding van
Bert van Meggelen, direkteur van de Academie
van Bouwkunst Rotterdam

VAN WEL

Aanvang: 20.00 uur

42 43

A New Architecture
Poster
Designers: Lorraine Wild, Whitney Lowe,
Lisa Nugent, Susan Parr
Design company: ReVerb/Los Angeles
Client: School of Architecture,
University of California at San Diego
USA, 1991

The Discourse of the Studio
Poster
Designers: J. Abbott Miller, Ellen Lupton
Design company: Design Writing Research
Printer: John Nichols
Client: American Collegiate Schools
of Architecture
USA, 1990

The Discourse of the Studio

CONFERENCE

1990 ACSA
Northeast Regional Meeting
School of Architecture
Princeton University

Friday, October 26 through
Saturday, October 27, 1990

A two-day conference devoted
to a discussion of the history,
current status of, and future
directions for the architectural
studio as both an educational
model and a determinant of
the language and practice of
architectural theory, criticism,
and design. Plenary speakers:

DAVID VAN ZANTEN
ROSEMARIE BLETTER
JUDITH WOLIN

EXHIBITION

The School of Architecture,
Princeton University,
is sponsoring an exhibition,
which will run concurrently
with the 1990 ACSA Northeast
Regional Meeting, of student
projects produced at schools in
the northeastern ACSA region.
The exhibition will consist of
projects from the 1989-90
academic year, representing
the most unique, successful,
and creative work produced
by students at each school.

The exhibition will run from
October 22 – November 9.

Submissions for papers and
panel discussions are due by
September 15, 1990.
Address inquiries to:
Alan Plattus
School of Architecture
Yale University
New Haven, CT 06520
tel: 203-432-2288
fax: 203-432-7175

To register, contact:
Cynthia Nelson
School of Architecture
Princeton University
Princeton, NJ 08544
tel: 609-258-5018
fax: 609-258-4740

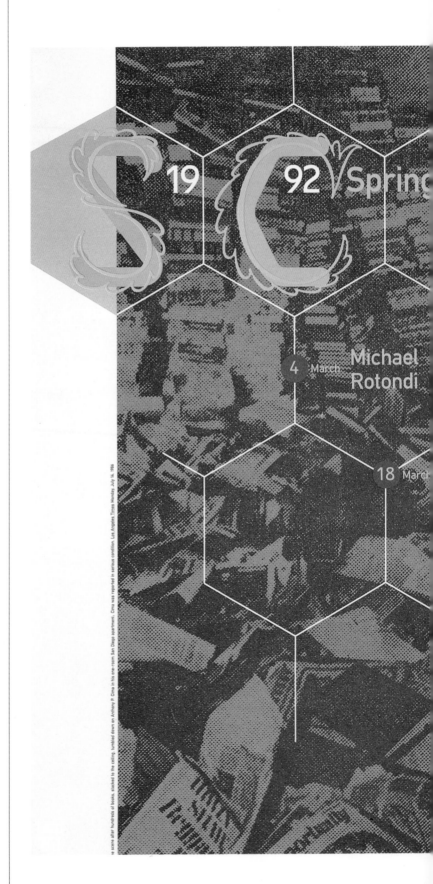

19 92 √ Spring

4 March

Michael
Rotondi

18 March

scene after hundreds of books, stacked to the ceiling, tumbled down on Anthony P. Cirma in his one-room San Diego apartment. Cirma was reported in serious condition. Los Angeles Times Monday, July 14, 1986

Spring 1992 Lecture Series
Architectural poster
Designer: Lorraine Wild
Design company: ReVerb/Los Angeles
Client: Southern California
Institute of Architecture
USA, 1992

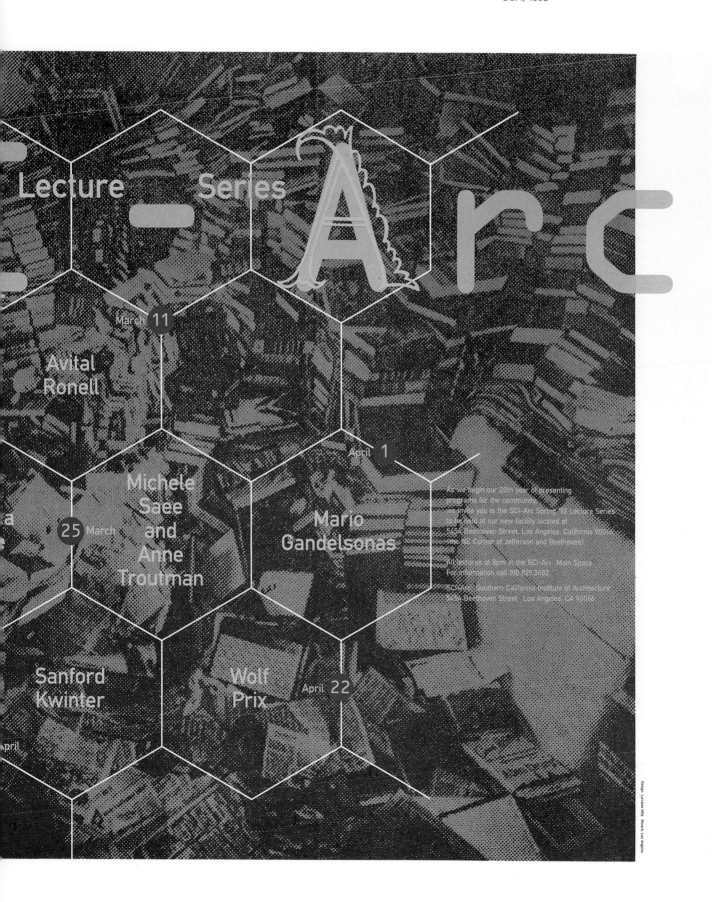

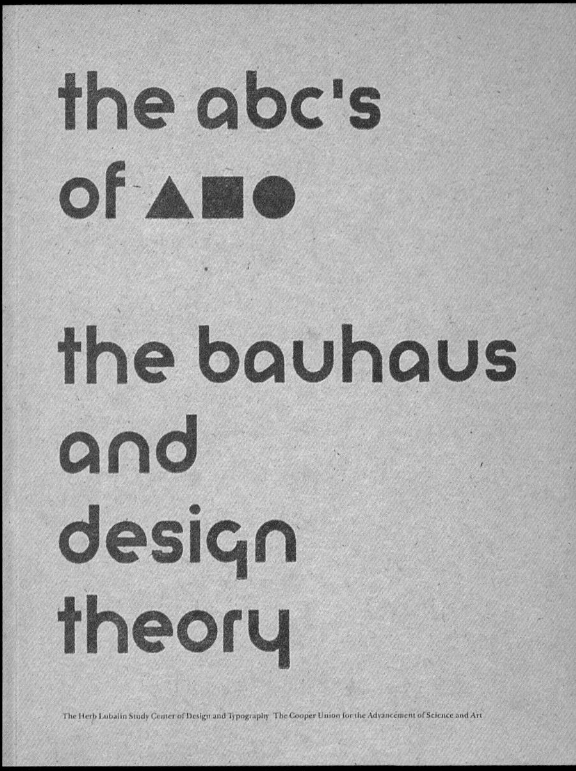

the abc's of ▲■●

the bauhaus and design theory

The Herb Lubalin Study Center of Design and Typography The Cooper Union for the Advancement of Science and Art

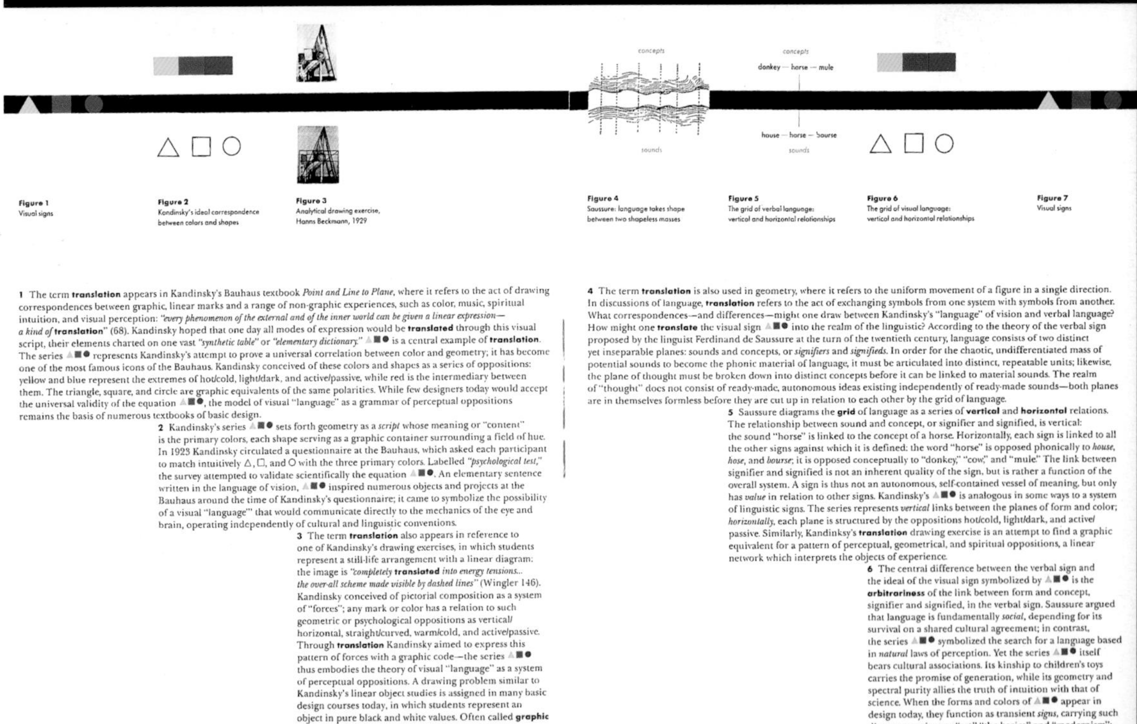

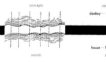

Figure 1
Visual signs

Figure 2
Kandinsky's ideal correspondence
between colors and shapes

Figure 3
Analytical drawing exercise,
Hanns Beckmann, 1929

Figure 4
Saussure: language takes shape
between two shapeless masses

Figure 5
The grid of verbal language:
vertical and horizontal relationships

Figure 6
The grid of visual language:
vertical and horizontal relationships

Figure 7
Visual signs

1 The term **translation** appears in Kandinsky's Bauhaus textbook *Point and Line to Plane*, where it refers to the act of drawing correspondences between graphic, linear marks and a range of non-graphic experiences, such as color, music, spiritual intuition, and visual perception: *"every phenomenon of the external and of the inner world can be given a linear expression— a kind of translation"* (68). Kandinsky hoped that one day all modes of expression would be **translated** through this visual script, their elements charted on one vast *"synthetic table"* or *"elementary dictionary."* ▲■● is a central example of **translation**. The series ▲■● represents Kandinsky's attempt to prove a universal correlation between color and geometry; it has become one of the most famous icons of the Bauhaus. Kandinsky conceived of these colors and shapes as a series of oppositions: yellow and blue represent the extremes of hot/cold, light/dark, and active/passive, while red is the intermediary between them. The triangle, square, and circle are graphic equivalents of the same polarities. While few designers today would accept the universal validity of the equation ▲■●, the model of visual "language" as a grammar of perceptual oppositions remains the basis of numerous textbooks of basic design.

2 Kandinsky's series ▲■● sets forth geometry as a *script* whose meaning or "content" is the primary colors, each shape serving as a graphic container surrounding a field of hue. In 1923 Kandinsky circulated a questionnaire at the Bauhaus, which asked each participant to match intuitively △, ☐, and ○ with the three primary colors. Labelled *"psychological test,"* the survey attempted to validate scientifically the equation ▲■●. An elementary sentence written in the language of vision, ▲■● inspired numerous objects and projects at the Bauhaus around the time of Kandinsky's questionnaire; it came to symbolize the possibility of a visual "language" that would communicate directly to the mechanics of the eye and brain, operating independently of cultural and linguistic conventions.

3 The term **translation** also appears in reference to one of Kandinsky's drawing exercises, in which students represent a still-life arrangement with a linear diagram: the image is *"completely translated into energy tensions... the over-all scheme made visible by dashed lines"* (Wingler 146). Kandinsky conceived of pictorial composition as a system of "forces"; any mark or color has a relation to such geometric or psychological oppositions as vertical/ horizontal, straight/curved, warm/cold, and active/passive. Through **translation** Kandinsky aimed to express this pattern of forces with a graphic code—the series ▲■● thus embodies the theory of visual "language" as a system of perceptual oppositions. A drawing problem similar to Kandinsky's linear object studies is assigned in many basic design courses today, in which students represent an object in pure black and white values. Often called **graphic translations**, these drawings combine the apparent objectivity of a photograph with the clarity of a letterform.

4 The term **translation** is also used in geometry, where it refers to the uniform movement of a figure in a single direction. In discussions of language, **translation** refers to the act of exchanging symbols from one system with symbols from another. What correspondences—and differences—might one draw between Kandinsky's "language" of vision and verbal language? How might one **translate** the visual sign ▲■● into the realm of the linguistic? According to the theory of the verbal sign proposed by the linguist Ferdinand de Saussure at the turn of the twentieth century, language consists of two distinct yet inseparable planes: sounds and concepts, or *signifiers* and *signifieds*. In order for the chaotic, undifferentiated mass of potential sounds to become the phonic material of language, it must be articulated into distinct, repeatable units; likewise, the plane of thought must be broken down into distinct concepts before it can be linked to material sounds. The realm of "thought" does not consist of ready-made, autonomous ideas existing independently of ready-made sounds—both planes are in themselves formless before they are cut up in relation to each other by the grid of language.

5 Saussure diagrams the **grid** of language as a series of **vertical** and **horizontal** relations. The relationship between sound and concept, or signifier and signified, is vertical: the sound "horse" is linked to the concept of a horse. Horizontally, each sign is linked to all the other signs against which it is defined: the word "horse" is opposed phonically to *house*, *hose*, and *hourse*; it is opposed conceptually to "donkey," "cow," and "mule." The link between signifier and signified is not an inherent quality of the sign, but is rather a function of the overall system. A sign is thus not an autonomous, self-contained vessel of meaning, but only has *value* in relation to other signs. Kandinsky's ▲■● is analogous in some ways to a system of linguistic signs. The series represents *vertical* links between the planes of form and color; *horizontally*, each plane is structured by the oppositions hot/cold, light/dark, and active/ passive. Similarly, Kandinsky's **translation** drawing exercise is an attempt to find a graphic equivalent for a pattern of perceptual, geometrical, and spiritual oppositions, a linear network which interprets the objects of experience.

6 The central difference between the verbal sign and the ideal of the visual sign symbolized by ▲■● is the **arbitrariness** of the link between form and concept, signifier and signified, in the verbal sign. Saussure argued that language is fundamentally *social*, depending for its survival on a shared cultural agreement; in contrast, the series ▲■● symbolized the search for a language based in *natural* laws of perception. Yet the series ▲■● itself bears cultural associations. Its kinship to children's toys carries the promise of generation, while its geometry and spectral purity allies the truth of intuition with that of science. When the forms and colors of ▲■● appear in design today, they function as transient *signs*, carrying such diverse meanings as "art," "the basics," and "modernism"; they are bound to cultural meaning by the act of quotation.

Appendix: The Gender of the Universal

Mike Mills

Western culture has constructed a dichotomy between what it labels as the "objective" quality of masculinity and the "subjective" quality of femininity. This mutually exclusive definition of gender has its analogue in Bayer's attempt to create a purely objective design which attempts to exclude, and deny, the presence of subjectivity. This appendix relates Sigmund Freud's theory of family power relations to Bayer's design methodology to show how these cultural beliefs about the meaning of masculine and feminine are developed, and to reveal that Bayer and Freud located reason and progress in the discipline and order personified by the father figure.

Mother: Freud believed that the mother "engulfs" the growing identity of the child with her nurturance. The child's total dependence on the mother in the first years of life renders him/her unable to differentiate the boundary between "self" and "mother." The child is unable to distinguish between its interior world and the exterior world. Freud argued that the child, especially the male child, must "repudiate" the mother in order to become autonomous and self-governing: "her nurturance threatens to re-engulf him with its reminder of helplessness and dependency; it must be corrected by his assertion of difference and superiority."[1] Freud labeled the mother as regressive: the child who remains bound to her is locked in a self-involved and narcissistic world.

History: Just as Freud believed the progress of the child depends on rejecting the mother, Bayer believed progress in design could only be achieved by rejecting the oppressive and "maternal" history of European culture. Modern design reacted to the self-aggrandizing, overly ornamented design of the nineteenth century: a tradition which Bayer believed to be deceitful, and—like the child who has not individuated from its mother—narcissistic. The customs of the past had to be rationalized. The need to differentiate from the mother, which Freud believed is integral to the male ego, is played out in the modernist rejection of and differentiation from the past: the child (modern design) rejects the mother (European history) and identifies with the father (American industry).

Father: Freud reinforces the common cultural belief which labels the mother as subjective and the father as objective. Freud believed that the father personifies objectivity because he brings external, social rules into the private, symbiotic relationship of the mother and child. The father grants the child a "way into the world" by asserting boundaries between the child and mother, and by inserting social norms the child must follow. He embodies an authority which Freud understood to be rational and progressive, and which the child both fears and admires. The child internalizes this "law of the father" in the form of the "super-ego": this is the agency which governs the ego, forcing the child to renounce the desire to stay united to the mother and enabling him/her to become self-governing.[2]

Progress: The demands of function work like a super-ego in the design of Bayer's Universal type. Just as the child becomes mature and responsible by internalizing the law of the father, Bayer believed that letterforms become socially responsible and progressive when the design internalizes the demands of function. Freud believed the child could only individuate from the mother by becoming objective, and similarly, Bayer believed typographic progress depended on finding objective, trans-cultural laws, which would guide the design out of the maternal arms of tradition and into the rational world of timeless laws. The dichotomy between mother and father in Freudian theory is echoed in Bayer's dichotomy between the "objective" law of progress and the "subjective" customs of the past.

1 Jessica Benjamin, *The Bonds of Love* (New York: Pantheon, 1988).

2 See Sigmund Freud, *Civilization and its Discontents* (New York: W. W. Norton, 1961).

Figure 1

Feminine: In 1896 social critic Gustav Le Bon reflected a popular prejudice when he stated that the modern crowd is irrational, volatile, and, "like women, it goes at once to extremes."[1] Similarly, the growth of machine-made commodities and such forms of mass entertainment as pulp fiction, advertising, and movies were labelled by defenders of "high" culture as an inauthentic, materialistic, and "*feminine*" threat to both traditional and modern forms of elite culture. "The swamp of big city life"... "The spreading ooze of massification," threatened to "engulf" the masculine high culture.[2] The boy's anxiety of being overwhelmed by the mother is re-enacted in high culture's fear of losing itself in the "false dreams" mass culture.

Figure 4

Subjectivity: The dichotomous thinking practiced by Bayer and Freud conflated dependence with irrationality. To be dependent on or influenced by the fluctuating and "whimsical" tastes of popular culture was to weaken the boundaries which make one autonomous and to contaminate the purity of detached reason. The over-abundance of fluctuating values of popular culture were treated as a threat to the stable, timeless authority of high culture and rational design. Design geared toward the undisciplined *appetite* of the masses rather than the refined *taste* of high culture was considered swamped in a materialisitic dream world reflecting the subjectivity and narcissism of the child who remains bound to its mother.

Masculine: While Universal type was designed for the masses, its appeal to (masculine) function over (feminine) form represents a correction of mass culture rather than an affirmation of it. The armature on which Universal was built functions like Freud's "rational" father: it represents a regulator that disciplines the letterform. The armature enabled the design to be based on objective rules that were exterior to the designer's personality and supposedly detached from the subjective and "feminine" realm of popular culture. It is this detachment which Freud believed the father embodies, and which Western culture aligns with masculinity. While this detachment is understood as neutral, it requires the *active* repudiation of subjectivity.

Figure 2

Objectivity: The ego boundaries which the child builds in the Oedipal stage make him/her autonomous from the mother. These boundaries are echoed in Bayer's dichotomy between popular culture and "functional" design, between a (regressive) history and a (progressive) future, and between (feminine) style and (masculine) rejection of style. The "neutral" objectivity which Bayer pursued can be reinterpreted as a reassertion of stable masculine ego boundaries and standards of "good" design in a world of rapidly changing values. Freud and Bayer invested belief in a science that is "premised on a radical dichotomy between subject and object and where all other experiences are accorded secondary 'feminine status.'"[3]

Figure 3

1 Gustave Le Bon, *The Crowd* (New York: Penguin, 1981) 50.

2 Andreas Huyssen, *After the Great Divide*, 52.

3 Evelyn Fox Keller, *Reflections on Gender and Science* (New Haven: Yale University Press, 1985) 87.

Figure 1 From Corbusier, *Towards a New Architecture*, 1931.
Figure 2 From Herbert Bayer, "towards a universal type," 1939-40
Figure 3 Self-portrait of Herbert Bayer's hand
Figure 4 From Herbert Bayer, "towards a universal type," 1939-40

Beyond ▲■●: Fractal Geometry

Alan Wolf

"Clouds are not spheres, mountains are not cones, coastlines are not circles... The number of distinct scales of length of natural patterns is for all practical purposes infinite. The existence of these patterns challenges us to study those forms that Euclid leaves aside as being 'formless,' to investigate the morphology of the 'amorphous'... Scientists will (I am sure) be surprised and delighted to find that not a few shapes they had to call *grainy, hydralike, in between, pimply, pocky, seaweedy, strange, tangled, tortuous, wiggly, wispy, wrinkled,* and the like, can henceforth be approached in rigorous and vigorous quantitative fashion."
Benoit Mandelbrot

Consider the apparently simple task of measuring the boundary of a fern. (We consider that the fern lies within a plane rather than having thickness, and thus is bounded by a curve.) Our measuring technique is to conform a piece of string to the perimeter of the fern as closely as possible. We then straighten the string and measure it's length with a ruler. As we use thinner and more flexible string, we are able to conform to smaller features of the perimeter, and our value for its length gradually increases.

We expect our values to converge to the "correct" length, but instead they seem to be growing to infinity! We could continue until our "string" reproduces the locations of individual atoms on the perimeter, but our interest here is in features that can be perceived by the senses or measured with macroscopic devices, so we will retain the fiction that our measurement process could have continued forever. We conclude that either the *perimeter* of the leaf is infinitely long, or that the question of its length is not well posed.

Our measurement technique suggests reasonable variants of the question, such as, "How long is a fern's perimeter when features no smaller than x are measured?" Since our eyes and other tools always have limited resolution, another reasonable question is "How long is a fern's perimeter when it is measured by x tool?" On a computer screen, for example, the size limitation is usually a screen "pixel." Thus a computer representation of a fern (such as the one shown here) is bounded by a finite number of pixels.

Now consider a cloud. The interior of a cloud is a "solid" three-dimensional object: it has length, width, and height. In this sense the interior of a cloud is like the interior of a balloon. The balloon's surface is (in our idealized discussion) perfectly smooth, and is thus an ordinary two-dimensional surface with a finite area. The cloud's surface, however, is wrinkly from its grossest features down to its microscopic structure. The cloud's *surface area* tends to infinity as the resolution of measurement increases.

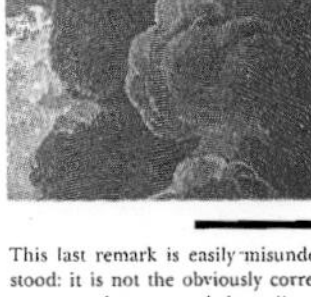

Mathematicians have quantified the wrinkliness of objects by modifying the standard definition of an object's dimension: in the new definition, points remain zero-dimensional, curves one-dimensional, and so on, but the *fractal dimension* of a cloud skin (from actual experimental measurements) has a value of about 2.3. Computer analysis of a photograph can provide such estimates. The value 2.3 suggests that a basically two-dimensional object is so wrinkled, it tends to act like a three-dimensional object.

This last remark is easily misunderstood: it is not the obviously correct statement that a crumpled two-dimensional piece of paper *occupies* a three-dimensional region of space (with some length, width, and height). What the statement *does* mean is that if the paper is wrinkled on all length scales, it tends to *densely fill* space like a solid three-dimensional object does: careful examination of the paper will not show that its "true" structure is two-dimensional, because the wrinkles never disappear at any level of scrutiny.

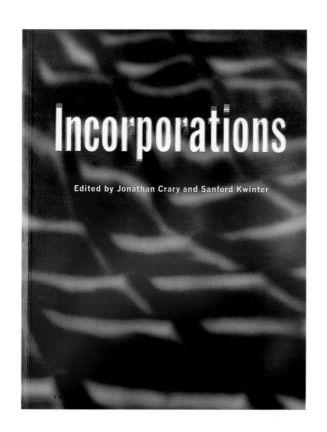

Incorporations

Edited by Jonathan Crary and Sanford Kwinter

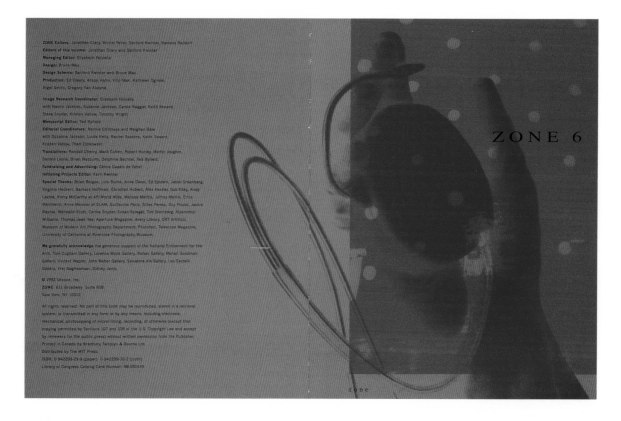

ZONE Editors: Jonathan Crary, Michel Feher, Sanford Kwinter, Ramona Naddaff.

Editors of this volume: Jonathan Crary and Sanford Kwinter

Managing Editor: Elizabeth Felicella

Design: Bruce Mau

Design Schema: Sanford Kwinter and Bruce Mau

Production: Ed Cleary, Alison Hahn, Viliji Maxi, Kathleen Oginski,
Nigel Smith, Gregory Van Alstyne.

Image Research Coordinator: Elizabeth Felicella
with Naomi Jackson, Suzanne Jackson, Carole Naggar, Keith Seward,
Steve Snyder, Kristen Vallow, Timothy Wright.

Manuscript Editor: Ted Byfield

Editorial Coordinators: Ronnie Childress and Meighan Gale
with Suzanne Jackson, Linda Kelly, Rachel Robbins, Keith Seward,
Kristen Vallow, Thad Ziolkowski.

Translations: Randall Cherry, Mark Cohen, Robert Hurley, Martin Joughin,
Donald Leslie, Brian Massumi, Delphine Bechtel, Ted Byfield.

Fundraising and Advertising: Céline Gazalli de Fabel

Initiating Projects Editor: Kern Kwinter

Special Thanks: Brian Boigon, Lois Burke, Anne Olson, Ed Epstein, Jacob Greenberg,
Virginia Heckert, Barbara Hoffman, Christian Hubert, Alex Kessler, Gus Kiley, Andy
Levine, Kerry McCarthy at AP/World Wide, Melissa Mathis, Jeffrey Meikle, Erica
Meinhardt, Anne Menicke at GLAM, Guillaume Paris, Gilles Peress, Guy Poulin, Jackie
Raynal, Wendolin Scott, Carina Snyder, Susan Spiegel, Tim Sternberg, Alyemobisi
Williams, Thomas Jean Yee; Aperture Magazine, Avery Library, ORT ArtInccio,
Museum of Modern Art Photography Department, Photofest, Telescope Magazine,
University of California at Riverside Photography Museum.

We gratefully acknowledge the generous support of the National Endowment for the
Arts, Tom Cogliani Gallery, Lorence Monk Gallery, Nohan Gallery, Mariah Goodman
Gallery, Vincent Wapler, John Weber Gallery, Salvatore Ala Gallery, Leo Castelli
Gallery, Vrej Baghoomian, Sidney Janis.

© 1992 Urzone, Inc.
ZONE 611 Broadway Suite 608
New York, NY 10012

Printed in Canada by Bradbury Tamblyn & Bourne Ltd.
Distributed by The MIT Press.
ISBN: 0-942299-29-9 (paper), 0-942299-30-2 (cloth)
Library of Congress Catalog Card Number: 98-051439

ZONE 6

zone

Zone 6: Incorporations
Book cover and spreads
Designers: Bruce Mau, Greg van Alstyne,
Nigel Smith, Alison Hahn, Kathleen Oginski
Design company: Bruce Mau Design
Client: Zone Books, New York
Canada, 1992

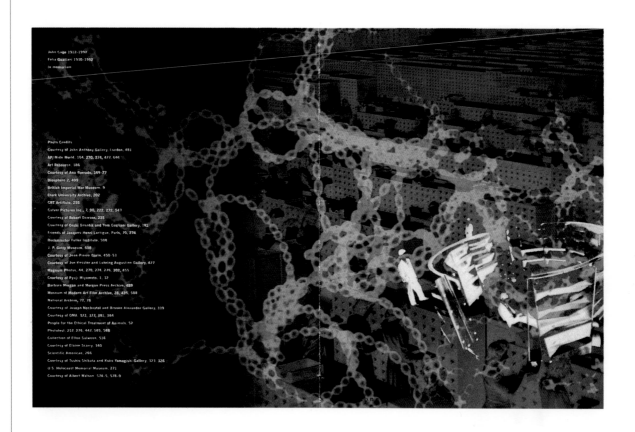

ZANDERS

						1	2
					7	8	9
10	11	12	13	14	15	16
17	18	19	20	21	22	23
24	25	26	27	28		

Our disk-shaped galaxy, the Milky Way, contains around 100 billion stars. Formed some 5 billion years ago, the Sun is situated on the inside edge of a spiral arm approximately 300 million billion kilometres from the centre. In taking 225 million years to complete a revolution, equivalent to one cosmic year, the Sun in its lifetime has circled the centre of the Milky Way just 25 times. A great power-house of fusion reactions, the Sun provides the Earth with over 100 million billion joules of energy every second.

Près de 100 milliards d'étoiles forment la Voie Lactée, notre galaxie en forme de disque. Le soleil, formé il y a 5 milliards d'ans, est situé sur la partie intérieure d'un bras en spirale, à environ 300 millions de milliards de kilomètres du centre. Pendant son existence, le soleil n'a fait que 25 fois le tour de la Voie Lactée, puisqu'il a besoin de 225 millions d'années, soit une année cosmique, pour réaliser une révolution complète. Le soleil, générateur puissant de réactions de fusion, fournit chaque seconde plus de 100 milliards de milliards de Joules d'énergie à notre terre.

Die Erde, vor ungefähr 4.800 Millionen Jahren geschaffen, brauchte 700 Millionen Jahre, um auf eine Temperatur unter der von kochendem Wasser abzukühlen. Erst dann begannen die Regenfälle, die die warmen, nährstoffreichen Seen bildeten, aus deren fruchtbarem Milieu schließlich das erste Leben hervorging. Die erste Spezies, die Blaualge, erschien vor ca. 800 Millionen Jahren. Etwa 465 Millionen Jahre später beherrschten die Dinosaurier die Erde. Die ersten menschenähnlichen Wesen tauchten erst vor nur 3 Millionen Jahren auf.

Created around 4,800 million years ago, the Earth took 700 million years to cool to a temperature below that of boiling water. Only then did the rains start, forming the warm nutrient-rich lakes that ultimately provided the fertile environment in which life began. The first species, the blue-green algae, appeared around 800 million years ago. Some 465 million years later the dinosaurs dominated the land. The earliest humanoids appeared a mere 3 million years ago.

La terre, créée il y a près de 4.800 millions d'années, eut besoin de 700 millions d'années pour refroidir à une température inférieure à celle de l'eau bouillante. Ce n'est qu'à cette époque qu'il commença à pleuvoir, et que furent formés les lacs riches en nutrients, base du début de la vie grâce à un environnement fertile. Les premières espèces, les algues bleues, apparurent il y a 800 millions d'années. Les dinosaures dominaient le monde quelque 465 millions d'années plus tard. Il n'y a que près de 3 millions d'années qu'apparurent les premiers humanoïdes.

Time. Machine. Future
1992 calendar: February, August
Designers: Mark Holt, Hamish Muir
Design company: 8vo
Client: Zanders
Great Britain, 1991

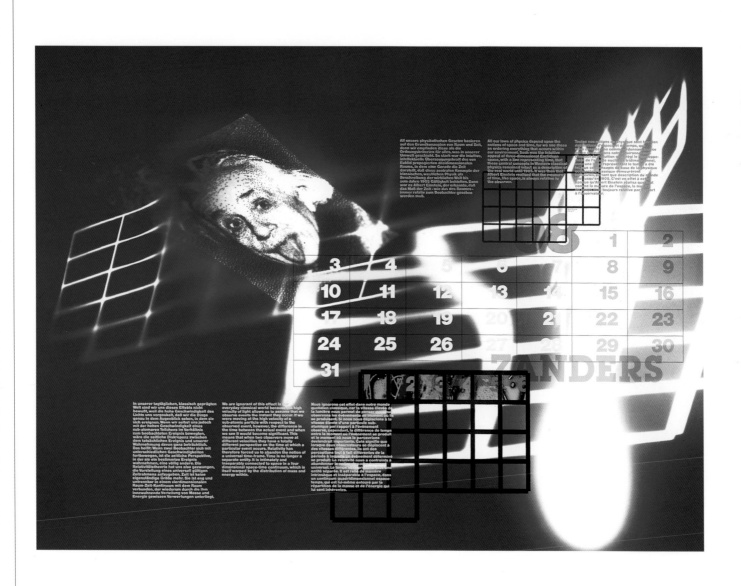

Museum poster series
Designers: Mark Holt, Hamish Muir
Design company: 8vo
Client: Museum Boymans-van Beuningen,
Rotterdam
Great Britain, 1990-91

Paviljoen Van Beuningen-de Vriese

nieuw

voor pre-industriële
gebruiksvoorwerpen,
kunstnijverheid en
industriële vormgeving

Museum Boymans-
van Beuningen Rotterdam

Bassheads

2045896
12R 6303

A. Side   B. Side   Additionals

Is there anybody out there?

Is there anybody out there? (extended).

Written by Deary / Murphy / Imre / Varitcus.
Produced by Bassheads / S. Imre.
Mixed by Deea & Ralphy.

Non verbal communication (extended).

Written by Murphy / Deary.
Produced by Bassheads.

Designed by 3a.

a *DECONSTRUCTION* record.
℗ 1991 the copyright in this sound recording is owned by EMI Records Ltd. © 1991 EMI Records Ltd.

a *DECONSTRUCTION* record.
132 Liverpool Road, London N1 1LA

Is there anybody out there?
Record sleeve (front and back)
Design director: Mark Farrow
Designers: Mark Farrow, Sian Cleaver,
Rob Petrie, Phil Sims
Design company: 3a
Client: Deconstruction Records
Great Britain, 1991

Mercatorplein
Poster
Design company: gebr de Jong
Client: Stadsdeel De Baarsjes
The Netherlands, 1992

K-klass
MPeople
Felix

DJ's

Tickets

Haçienda. Tuesday September 15th.

Mike Pickering, Daniele Davoli,
Danny Rampling and Alistair Cooke.

Piccadilly Box Office,
HMV,
Haçienda.
£7.

*another steamy night out with **DECONSTRUCTION**.*

Concert posters
Design director: Mark Farrow
Designers: Mark Farrow, Rob Petrie, Phil Sims
Design company: Farrow
Client: Deconstruction Records
Great Britain, 1992

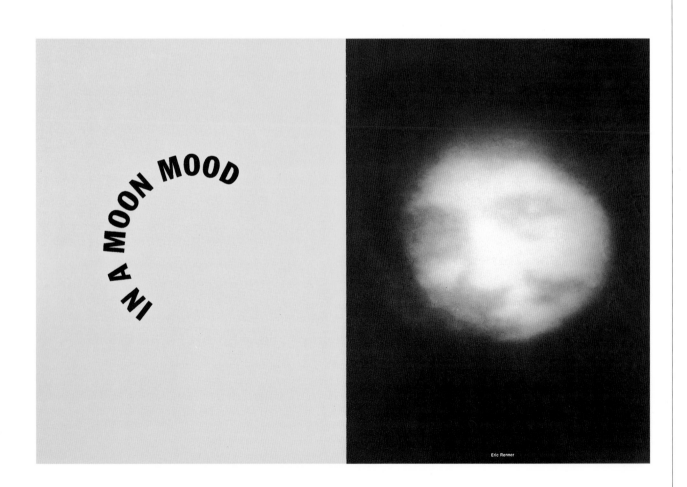

IN A MOON MOOD

Eric Renner

Interview
Magazine spread
Designers: Tibor Kalman, Richard Pandiscio
Design company: M&Co
Photographer: Eric Renner
Client: *Interview*
USA, January 1991

Self-promotional poster
Designers: Paul Neale, Andrew Stevens,
Nigel Robinson
Design company: Graphic Thought Facility
Self-published
Great Britain, 1992

Style is the clothing of any visual communication. Used thoughtfully it can enhance and reinforce the message, at it's worst it is simply visual noise cloaking a lack of any real substance. Through lack of thought or misplaced self-promotion, designers continue to rely upon a pre-concieved personal style to satisfy any brief regardless of its relevance. At GTF, each job is appraised, every solution a considered one. Observation, exploration of processes, a genuine understanding of graphic design's function and above all the application of thought are all part of our composition, GTF's Style.

The Salisbury, Grand Parade, Green Lanes, London, N4 1JX, Great Britain.
Telephone 081 809 4672. Facsimile 081 341 2215.

GRAPHIC THOUGHT FACILITY

RSC Fringe Festival '91
The Last Days of Don Juan
Theatre posters
Designer: Paul Neale, Andrew Stevens,
Nigel Robinson
Design company: Graphic Thought Facility
Client: Royal Shakespeare Company
Great Britain, 1991

Acts of Faith
Theatre poster
Designer: A. Arefin
Photographer: Anthony Oliver
Client: Institute of Contemporary Arts, London
Great Britain, 1992

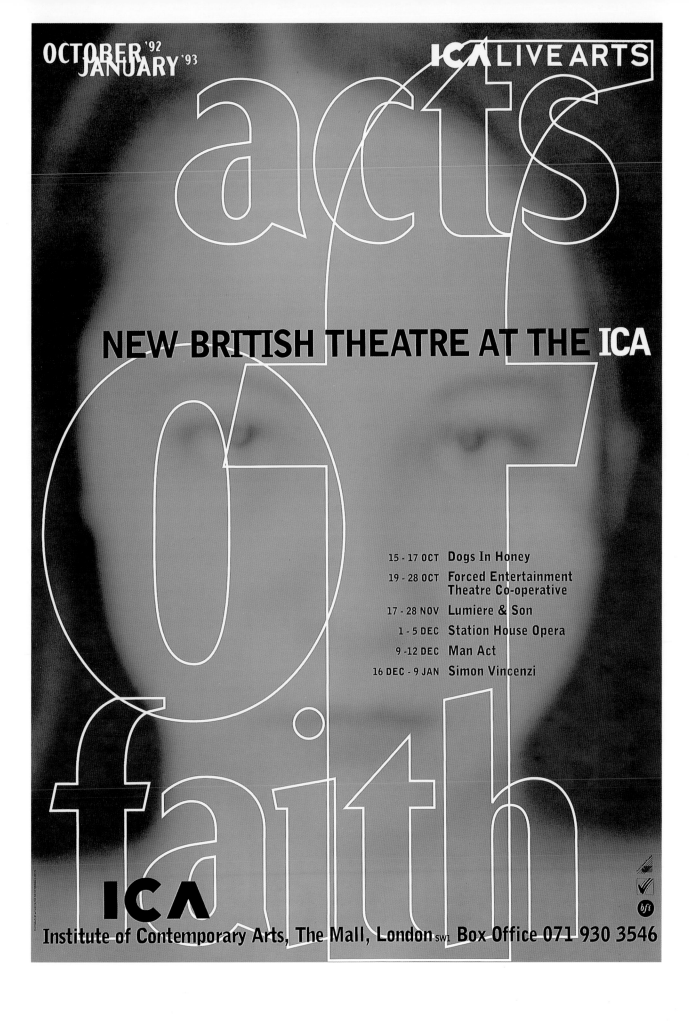

Economische Structuur 1993
Calendar: January, May
Designers: Jacques Koeweiden, Paul Postma
Design company: Koeweiden Postma
Photographer: YANi
Client: Ministry of Economic Affairs
The Netherlands, 1992

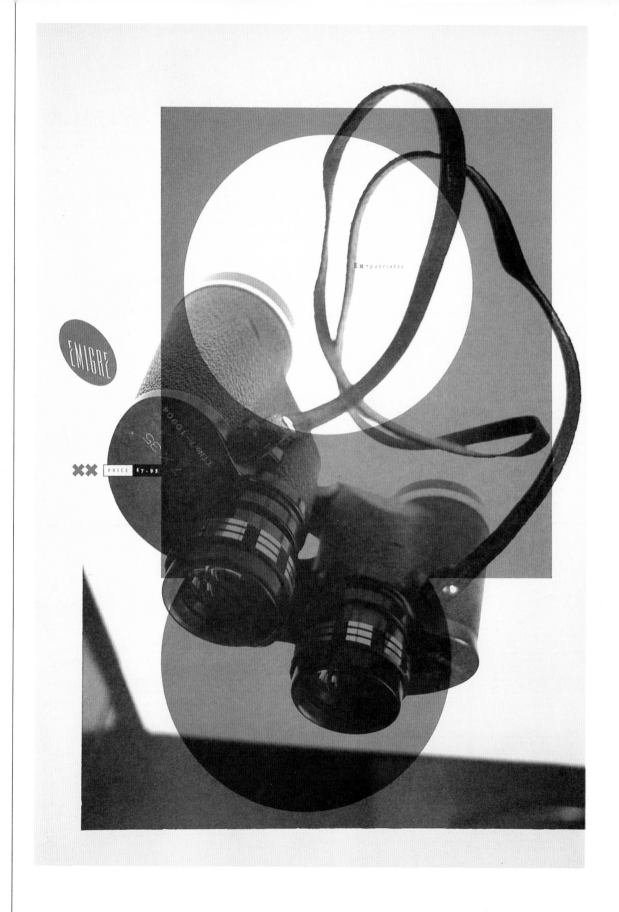

EMIGRE

Ex·patriates

XX PRICE $7·95

Emigre
Magazine covers
Designer: Rudy VanderLans
Design company: Emigre Graphics
Self-published
USA, 1991, 1992

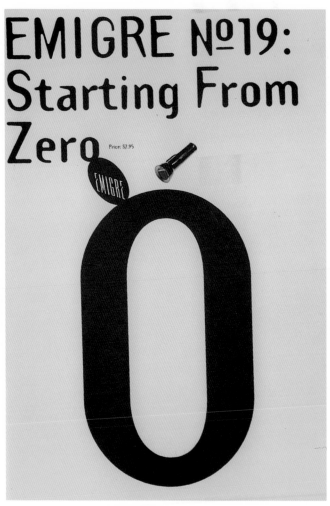

Richard III
Civil War Events
Festival posters
Designers: Andy Altmann, David Ellis,
Christopher Priest
Design company: Why Not Associates
Photographer: Nick Georghiou
Client: Hull City Council
Great Britain, 1992

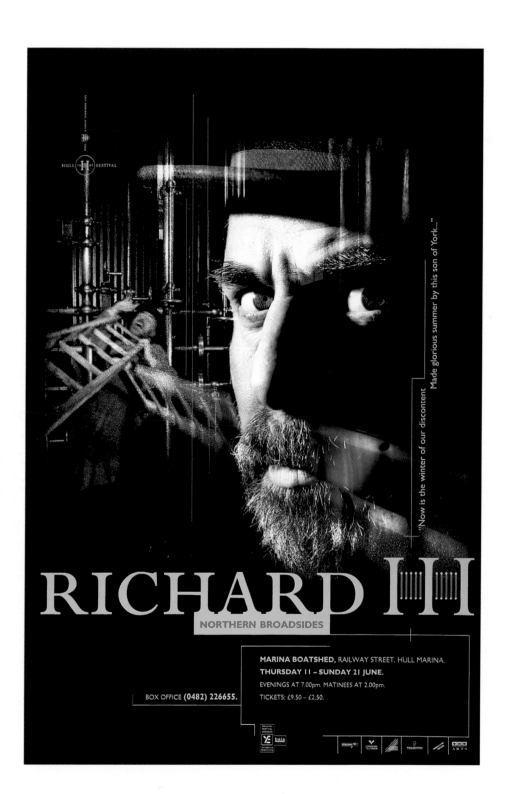

HULL IS JUSTLY PROUD OF ITS HISTORIC REFUSAL
TO ALLOW CHARLES I TO ENTER THE WALLS,
IN APRIL 1642. A SIGNIFICANT TURNING POINT
IN ROYAL POPULARITY, IT JUSTIFIES THE CLAIM:

**HULL – BIRTHPLACE OF
THE CIVIL WAR 1642 – 1992**

CIVIL WAR

HULL 1992
FESTIVAL   HULL – A GREAT YORKSHIRE CITY

events

april 11 - may 31	**Arms and Armour Exhibition**	town docks museum
april 15	**Cromwell Film**	Ferens Art Gallery
april 23	**Witchfinder General Film**	hull film theatre
april 17 - 23	**Hull Flower and Church Arts Festival**	holy trinity church
april 23	**Civic Service with Lord Tonypandy**	holy trinity church
april 25	**Beverley Gate Refusal Re-enactment**	beverley gate
april 25	**The Governors Reception Party**	the maltings
april - december	**Hull in the 17th Century**	wilberforce house
june 15 - 19	**Hull 1642: Living History Events**	schools
june 16 - 27	**Hull City Play**	city hall
june 20 - 21	**Re-enactment of Civil War Battle**	city site
july 11 - 12	**Wilberforce House: July 1642**	wilberforce house

PRINCIPAL
FESTIVAL
SPONSOR

Yorkshire
Electricity

organized in association with
the English Civil War Society.

ARTS

photography: jeremy hall (royal armouries), neil holmes
design: why not associates

most events are free
for further details telephone
Hull Festival hotline on 0482 223344

the inventivespirit

NEW DESIGN FROM **BRITAIN** | DES NOUVELLES CONCEPTIONS DE **GRANDE–BRETAGNE**
NIEUW DESIGN UIT **GROOT–BRITTANNIE**

AUTOWORLD BRUSSELS
PARC DU CINQUANTENAIRE 11 · JUBELPARK 11,
1040 BRUXELLES · BRUSSEL.
13.10.92. - 06.11.92. 10.00am - 5.00pm.

The Inventive Spirit
Exhibition poster
Designers: Andy Altmann, David Ellis,
Christopher Priest
Design company: Why Not Associates
Photographer: Rocco Redondo
Client: The Foreign and Commonwealth Office
Great Britain, 1992

Animation at The Mill
Promotional Poster
Designer: Siobhan Keaney
Photographer: Robert Shackleton
Client: The Mill
Great Britain, 1992

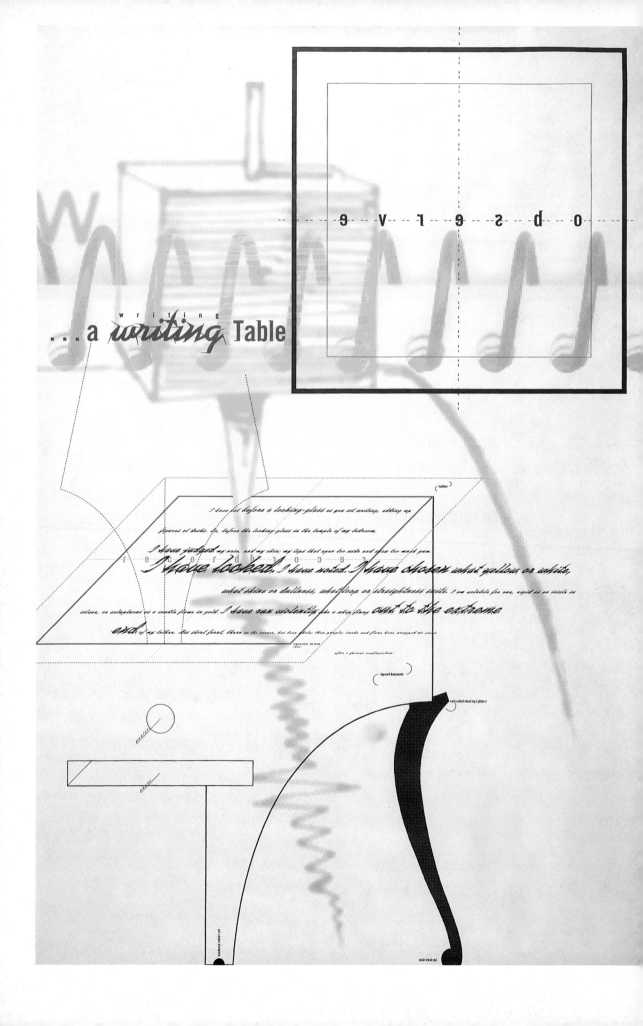

observe

...a **writing** Table

record

A Writing Table
Poster
Designer/illustrator: Mark D. Sylvester
Design company: Point
Client: Abigail J. Shachat
USA, 1992

30 years Amnesty International
Poster
Designer: Jan Marcus Jancourt
Client: Amnesty International/Wabnitz
Editions
USA, 1991

A Writing Table
Poster
Designer/illustrator: Mark D. Sylvester
Design company: Point
Client: Abigail J. Shachat
USA, 1992

30 years Amnesty International
Poster
Designer: Jan Marcus Jancourt
Client: Amnesty International/Wabnitz
Editions
USA, 1991

Growing Points
Promotional poster
Designer: Lisa Taft Sylvester
Design company: Point
Photographer: Lisa Taft Sylvester
Client: Great Lakes Color Printers
USA, 1991

Art for Life
Poster/invitation
Designer: Allen Hori
Photographers: Allen Hori, Jaymes Leahy
Client: Aid for AIDS Research, Detroit
USA, 1990

APRIL

APRIL

IN

7:00PM

APRIL GREIMAN
APRIL 10, 1991

DESALLE AUDITORIUM, CRANBROOK ACADEMY OF ART

THEY
WILL COME

SPONSORED BY AIGA DETROIT & CHAMPION INTERNATIONAL

THIS EVENT IS PART OF THE SERIES "CHAMPIONS OF DESIGN" WHICH IS MADE POSSIBLE IN PART BY A GRANT FROM CHAMPION INTERNATIONAL

April in April
Lecture poster
Designer: James A. Houff
Photographer: Paul Price
Client: American Institute of
Graphic Arts, Detroit
USA, 1991

Promotional poster
Designer: James A. Houff
Client: Typocraft Printers
USA, 1990

GUIDE **2**

Ohio

MEDIA **EQUIPMENT**

Ohio Arts Council

⬇

Access
sites

Guide to Ohio Media Equipment
Access Sites
Brochure cover
Designer/photographer: Crit Warren
Design company: Schmeltz + Warren
Client: Ohio Arts Council
USA, 1991

Towards College in Ohio 91-92
Brochure cover
Designer/photographer: Crit Warren
Design company: Schmeltz + Warren
Client: The Ohio College Association
USA, 1990

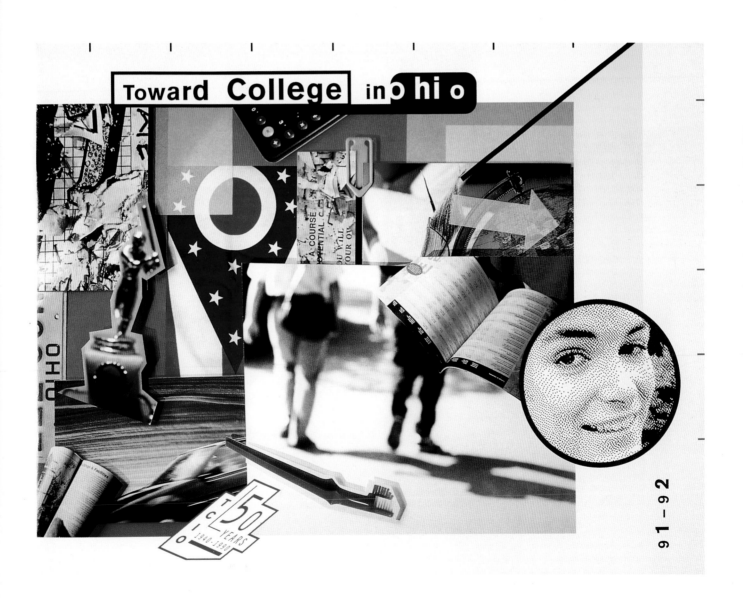

Man ist
was Man
was
sieht

TYPE 1

Balance

72

design:Weber(john)

16201-B
PC-31077

$1.59

ACT NOW!

Fill in the coupon and start your
membership in this remarkable
book club.

1   2   3   4
5   6   7

membership requires advance deposit of $10.00.

OPEN HERE

241

FERRINGTON

Guitars

Chris
DIFFORD

Chris Difford is a guitarist, singer, and songwriter with the British band Squeeze. Working in collaboration with fellow band member Glenn Tilbrook, Difford helped develop the distinctively humane sound and colorful working-class imagery that characterize Squeeze's music.

1981 | 15½ inches

Spruce top maple body and neck ebony fretboard

Chris saw some of the guitars I'd made for Elvis Costello when his band Squeeze was opening for Elvis during a show, and eventually we got together to collaborate on the designs for two guitars. This small guitar was made to look like an acoustic version of a Rickenbacker-style electric like the kind John Lennon used to play.

It was a little bit tricky to do, because the curves in the points were so sharp that I had to use solid blocks of wood to make the front. You can't tell what I did when you look at it, though, because I made it appear as if I had actually bent the wood to fit those really sharp angles.

Ferrington Guitars
Book cover and spreads
Designers: Nancy Skolos, Thomas Wedell
Design company: Skolos/Wedell
Photographer: Thomas Wedell
Client: Callaway Editions
USA, 1992

nevillebrody For designers and readers of the London-based magazines Arena or The Face, Neville Brody needs no introduction. The original bad-boy typographer, the visual interpreter of London's early Punk Rock scene, the champion of a visionary personal style — Brody has risen to prominence at a meteoric pace, revolutionizing the look of editorial design, advertising and typography along the way. Brody has also shouldered the burden of rapid success. Those at the top of the design profession are rampantly plagiarized and then criticized for their association with a watered-down trend. Introspective but not bitter, Brody has steadfastly moved on. When reached by phone at 8:00pm on a Sunday night, he was finishing up a project in his studio, rushing to catch a late flight to Bonn, and flat out sick with the flu. This not withstanding, he couldn't have sounded more high-spirited, as if nothing could slow him down. Are you always going at 100 miles per hour? No. . . but I do work all the time. If you're not obsessed, I believe, you're not going to get any really good work out of yourself. Are you obsessed by your work? Yes, completely. Not obsessive, mind you, but completely immersed. Recently, I read something in Emigré magazine that I wanted to ask you about. There is a line about you having taken "safe refuge in the International Style." What did you think when you read that? I wanted to reply to that, particularly since, two pages later, there is a comment that says something to the effect that "Neville Brody should have packed it in when he was still successful. . ." What can you say? Concerning the "safe refuge" remark, I want to go on record as saying that it's complete ____ ____ ____ ____ . Modernism isn't a "safe refuge." My work for Arena, for example, was a modernist statement because it was a necessary reaction to everything that had gone before. There had been such a desperate search for the new that anything different became valid, even if it was completely meaningless. So the contrast between The Face and Arena was an obvious counter-reaction? Exactly. I wasn't saying, "Well, we've had our fun, now let's return to modernism." That wasn't my idea at all. Instead, I was saying: "Let's get back to basics and really think about what we're doing, think about the power of simplicity. With Arena, I wanted to show that we've all become obsessed with style for style's sake. Instead, we should return to basics and start thinking again. I also wanted to show that it was possible to use modernism as an emotive way of communicating. It sounds as though for a while there you became pretty disenchanted with the design scene. At the end of the 1980s, design had become a commodity of its own, which I've never agreed with. When design stops making people think, it becomes redundant. Design is supposed to be a way of translating ideas. It does not function well when it stands alone. Wasn't your switch to modernism actually a radical idea for its time? Yes, but like most radical ideas, it was misinterpreted. Regardless of what others may think, I do not believe in a return to modernism for its own sake or as a stylistic statement — only as a way to help us think about what we should be doing and as a way to reexamine where our responsibilities lie. For me it served as a way to ask: "What is the role of design in society?" Do you think that people are misinterpreting your backlash by calling it a retreat? Yes, completely. But as a designer, you have to keep changing. Regardless of all this criticism, you sound extremely busy. Yes, thankfully, we have a lot of clients at the moment. Yet, strangely, only one is British and none are American. Really? Yes. Most of our work is in Germany, Japan, France, Holland and Spain. I can't explain why, it just worked out that way. It's bizarre, really. What explains the shift away from Britain and America? By the nature of our work, we tend to gravitate toward societies with more forward-thinking people — people who are more willing to take risks. There's also the question of money. To give some idea, our one British client — a shelf company — elected to pay us with shelves rather than cash. What's your rate? Seventeen shelves per day. The way we see it, you can never have enough shelves.

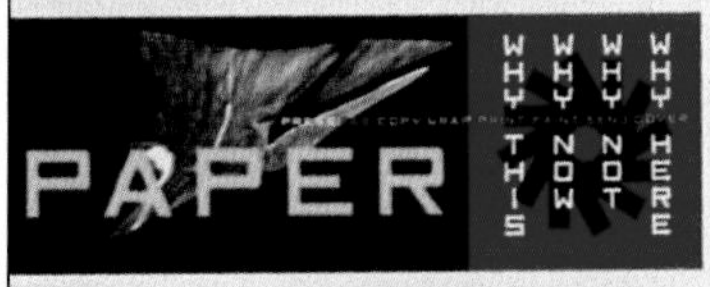

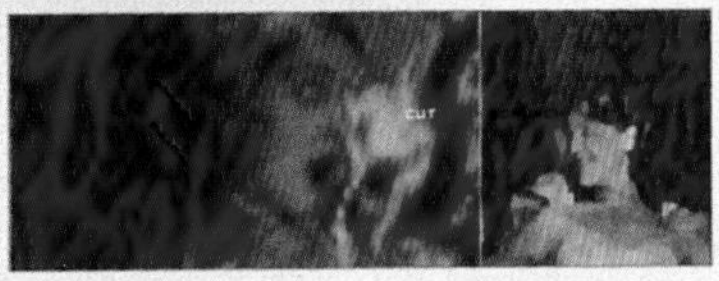

NEVILLE • MALCOLM

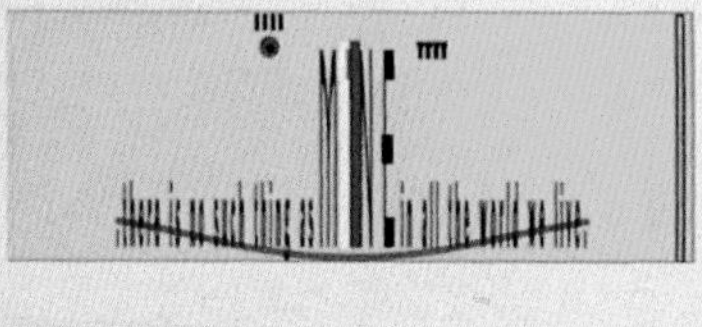

RICK rickvalicenti RICK • KATHERINE

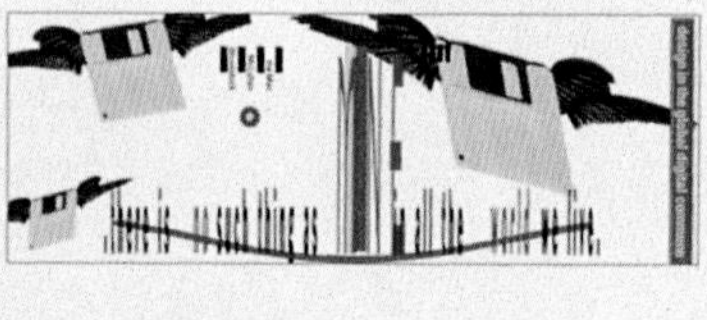

The word Thirst signifies both the name and the impassioned creative drive behind a small studio founded in Chicago by Rick Valicenti in 1988. Champions of a deeply personal approach to graphic design, Valicenti and his collaborator Michael Giammanco have provoked the design establishmen
artistic, cheeky experiments that have quickly proven to be a legitimate contribution to design's discourse. Before long, gestures that were used expressively (or ironically) in the Thirst vocabulary made their way into a rash of portfolios, where their witticisms have been largely misinterpreted. T
however, wasn't standing still. When we caught up with Valicenti at O'Hare International airport, he was keen to discuss cake decoration, Attitude Design, and the inspiration behind the Exquisite Corpse experiment you have before you. How has Thirst forged its distinctive, audacious style in the n
of heartland America? The only way I can answer that is to say we're just being ourselves. I'm just being me. And that's not said out of arrogance or false pride — it's just all I know. Not being trained as a graphic designer, I've had to learn how to absolutely trust my instincts. What's your impression
the state of graphic design today? A lot of the #@*% I see out there is so jive ... Well, don't print that. Let's just say a lot of design is derivative, and at this point a lot of it has become derivative of itself, so it's a self-perpetuating spiral. I've become so bored with attitude. I'd rather be on the sideline cal
spade a spade. But you're not on the sideline! At this year's AIGA conference you were at the top of the roster ... Yes, but I'm only servicing a small group of design-driven clients. So in that sense I'm not in a position where I'm supposed to appeal to the mass-market. There's a great deal of freed
remaining small and running a lean organization. Do the Thirst imitators drag you down? They are of little concern except when they have a negative impact on my business development efforts. In any case if someone copies my typographic gestures, they may not be adopting the reasons for empl
those gestures. So how do you stay ahead of the pack? The only way is through provocation. By revealing levels of thinking that are much more in-depth than anything anyone had expected. People are looking for the cake decoration and they aren't going to find it. As I see it, the trap for a designer g
when he or she starts doing work to fulfill someone else's expectations. Then the designer become static. Thank you very much! That's the story exactly. The primary challenge is to fulfill only your own expectations; for me that often includes poking some fun — even at myself. What was your inspi
for this Exquisite Corpse project? What I told Michael, my partner, was that this project was like tribes sending smoke signals out to each other. We're saying, hey, we're having some fun over here, what's going on over there? And the part that's so exciting to me is to think that designers who respe
another can relinquish their own work to one of their peers, and then embrace someone else's work. What was the smoke signal you sent out? It's a very simple thing, partly a self-portrait in type, created from a line from Buddha: THERE IS NO SUCH THING AS MINE IN ALL THE WC
To me this quote represented what we are doing, because here I was creating a design on a disk that I'm passing along to Katherine, who will make her mark, and then send it on to Neville, who will transform it again. I wanted to make a statement that what I was sending out was not mine, and the
person should feel free to do with it as they please. To me it's an exhilarating and unnerving way to exchange a message. All egos are checked at the door on this project? Absolutely. Everyone has said nothing is theirs. Helvetica or Franklin Gothic don't belong to any one designer; the use of warm re
black doesn't belong to any one dogma; and the use of arrows doesn't belong to the vernacular. It's all out there for us to use as communication. That is the spirit of this whole project. What do you hope will come of this Exquisite Corpse experiment? My feeling is that if seven designers can work togeth
this level, then there's no reason why those seven can't join up with seven others and so on. My most optimistic goal is for the world of electronic communication to be made a bit smaller, and for design collaboration to become a bit wider as a result of this global network.

RICK • KATHERINE • NE

ERIK • PAUL • LINDA • R

erikspiekermann

In the heart of Berlin, adjacent to what used to be the symbolic and actual Wall of separation between East and West, Erik Spiekermann's twelve-year-old firm MetaDesign holds the distinction of being the largest graphic design office in Germany. With eighteen employees, the firm services a range of public and private institutions throughout the re-united country; occasionally, an overseas client in need of "a token Kraut," to use Spiekermann's term, comes knocking at MetaDesign's door. Yet despite his cultural jabs, the designer happily embraces Teutonic stereotypes. His greatest professional joy, he proclaims, comes of creating order where once there was none. Spiekermann's discovery of a Corbusian Golden Mean within the dimensions of this very page, for example, serves as a telling indication of his quest for exactitude. The obvious question for a designer — or anyone — living in Berlin right now is, What's going on? What is happening as your city undergoes such enormous changes. The problem I have in responding is that I'm too close to the situation. Even though I'm acutely aware that this is a historic moment, and that nothing like this has ever happened before, it's not easy to describe. It's not every day that a political system that has been in existence for forty years suddenly disappears. Yes, and all of the sudden I can walk 100 yards from the door of my office and I'm in East Berlin. It's odd, because (over there) everything looks different, feels different, smells different, and the people are all different, but geographically there is no difference any more. It's quite difficult for the human imagination to comprehend. Once we were two islands, and now there is no physical distance between us.

And yet you are part of the same culture, you all speak the same language. That makes it even worse. We're two countries divided by a common tongue. If (th
Germans) spoke a different language, then it would be obvious and it would be easier to assimilate these kinds of cultural differences. Has the unity of Berlin resulted
new commissions for you? One of our projects at the moment is the signage system for a major subway station in Berlin, half of which was closed for forty years wh
city was divided. This is a great project because it's a public service that is truly needed, which is the type of work that I view as ideal. I would feel slightly superfluou
we did were paper promotions. You once were quoted as saying that you weren't Neville Brody and you weren't changing the face of typography. What did you me
that? I meant I'm not really interested in visuals. I'm not really interested in what things loo
I like solving problems. I'm a structuralist — I like to get the structure of a problem work
and then hand it to someone else who will then visualize it. Could you describe this process?
people the ingredients. I say this is the grid, these are the typefaces, and here are the hiera
But I don't do the layout. I give people the box of tricks and they go and do the visuals. That's unusual. In my experience I find that graphic designers work much
visually than verbally. My style is reductionist simply because I haven't got the generosity, or the verve, you might say, to arrange elements across a spread so that the
natural, which is something I very much admire in Neville, but I can't do. So you see, I'm not an artist. Then it's beginning to make sense why you were so interested
formal components of this assignment. I have to tell you that you were the only one involved in this project who took one look at the dimensions of this page and discov
Golden Mean based on Le Corbusier's system of proportional measurements! I always break down the spatial relationships of a page, and in this case I found that the measurement from one side to the other is the square root of eight. Don't ask me why I found that! I guess its my preoccupation with proportion, grids and the division of pages, which I find quite magical and cabalistic. So your concern is with structures that are invisible. Well somebody has to be concerned with those things. It's the grammar of design — it exists whether you recognize it or not. And yet there is something about the rules of grammar that most designers prefer to avoid. Maybe it's my German brain, but I like to know about these rules and apply them. In my opinion it's the only way you can break them, which I also enjoy doing.

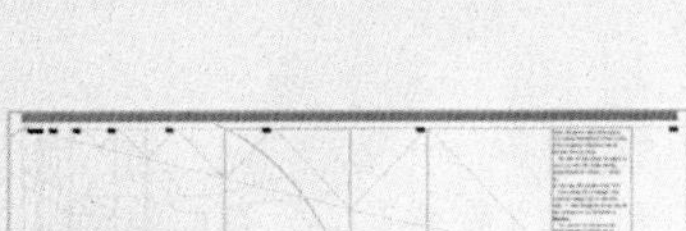

ERIK

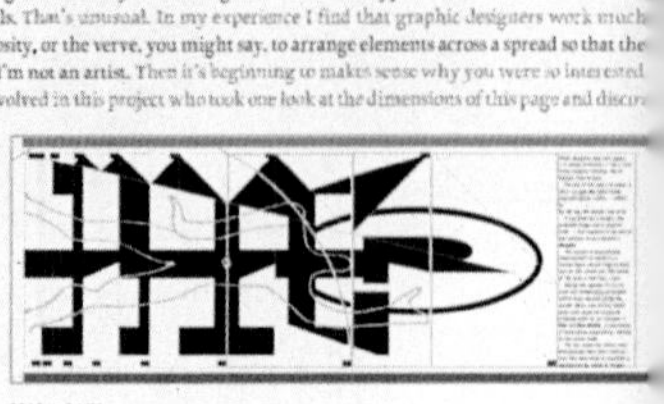

ERIK • PAUL

Electronic Exquisite Corpse
Brochure spreads showing three-way design collaborations
Art director: Rick Valicenti
Design company: Thirst
Designers: Neville Brody > Malcolm Enright > Katherine McCoy
Rick Valicenti > Katherine McCoy > Neville Brody
Erik Spiekermann > Paul Sych > Linda van Deursen, Armand Mevis
Client: Gilbert Paper
USA, 1991

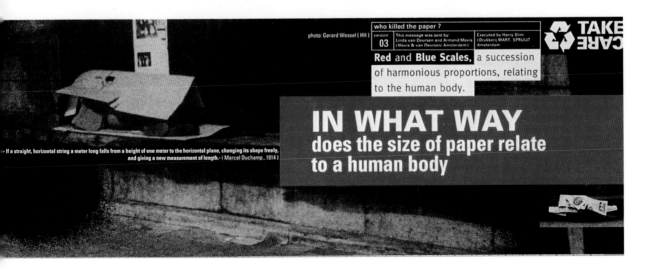

Luigi *Pirandello* festival

festival

Theater F R A S C A T I

aanvangstijden zie: Nesjournaal december

telefonisch reserveren (020) 26 68 66

vrijdag **tm** zaterdag
14.12.90 22.12.90

Theater Frascati
en de Engelenbak
Nes 63 en 71
gesponserd door:
&ANDERSSON
LUBBERS
en Atelier Sericus
zeefdruk t 020 - 24 92 99

Luigi Pirandello Festival
Poster
Designers: Jacques Koeweiden, Paul Postma
Client: Theater Frascati, Amsterdam
The Netherlands, 1990

Trap 5
Dance poster
Designers: Jacques Koeweiden, Paul Postma
Design company: Koeweiden Postma
Photographer: YANi
Client: Dans Produktie, Amsterdam
The Netherlands, 1991

De Haagse Zomer
(The Hague Summer)
Festival posters
Designers: Ben Faydherbe, Wout de Vringer
Design company: Faydherbe/De Vringer
Photographer: Jordi Bover (1989)
Client: Het Gebeuren
The Netherlands, 1989, 1990, 1991

[LATITUDE]

Writing

THROUGH THE EDGE

Saturday, May 7

A ONE-DAY CONFERENCE SPONSORED BY THE
... CENTER FOR DESIGN ... EXPLORE THE
...S IN CREATIVE THINKING

Moderator
TODD LIEF

ARCHITECTURE
STANLEY TIGERMAN
ART
MR. IMAGINATION
GRAPHIC DESIGN
ED FELLA
MUSIC
SHULAMIT RAN
PRODUCT DESIGN
DAVID GRESHAM
WRITING
KARRIE JACOBS

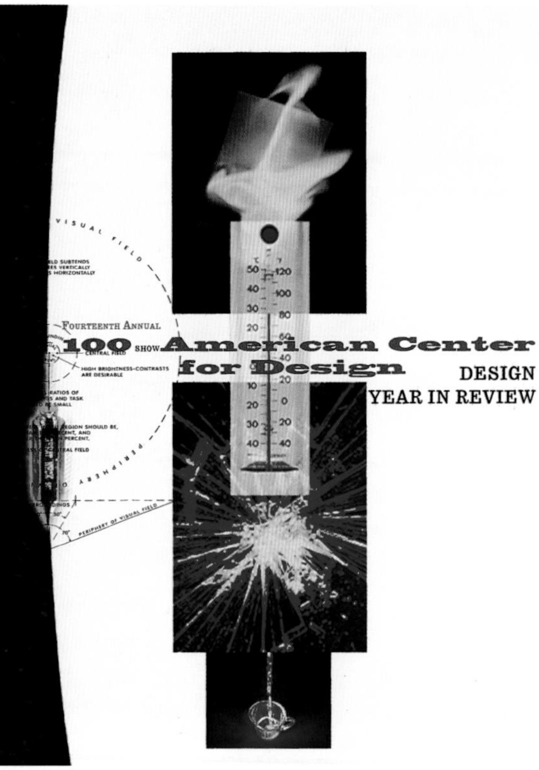

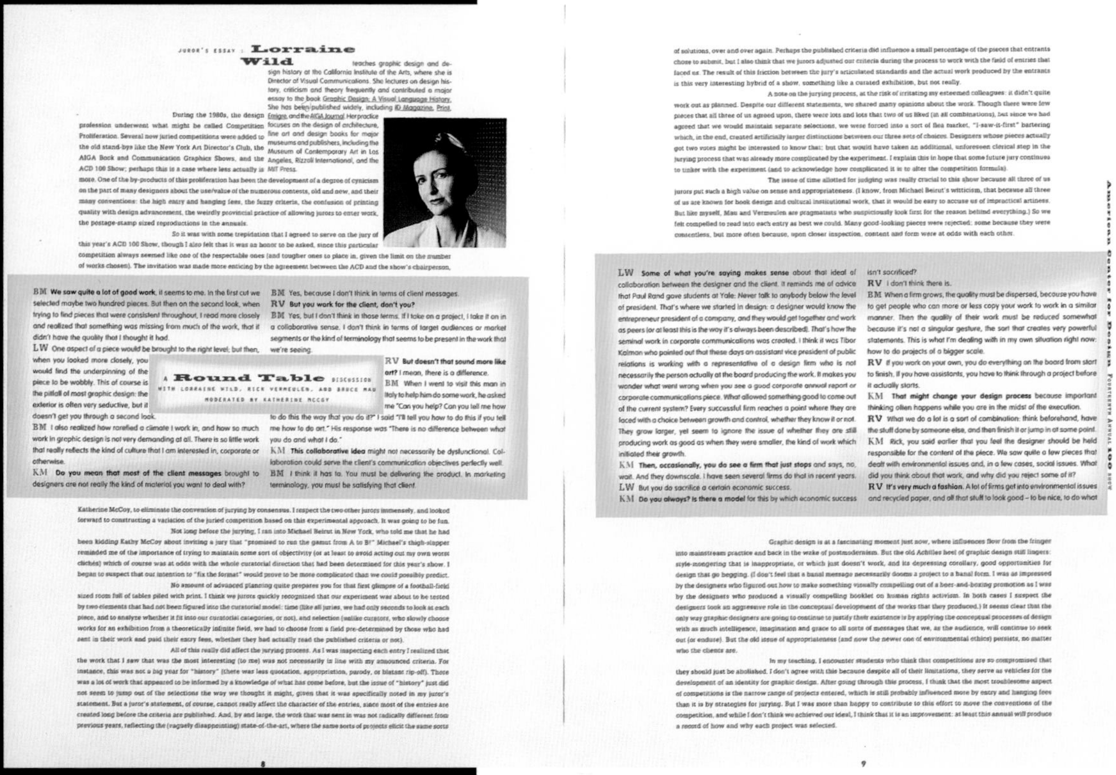

JUROR'S ESSAY : **Lorraine Wild** teaches graphic design and design history at the California Institute of the Arts, where she is Director of Visual Communications. She lectures on design history, criticism and theory frequently and contributed a major essay to the book Graphic Design: A Visual Language History. She has been published widely, including ID Magazine, Print, Emigre, and the AIGA Journal. Her practice focuses on the design of architecture, fine art and design books for major museums and publishers, including the Museum of Contemporary Art in Los Angeles, Rizzoli International, and the MIT Press.

During the 1980s, the design profession underwent what might be called Competition Proliferation. Several new juried competitions were added to the old stand-bys like the New York Art Director's Club, the AIGA Book and Communication Graphics Shows, and the ACD 100 Show; perhaps this is a case where less actually is more. One of the by-products of this proliferation has been the development of a degree of cynicism on the part of many designers about the use/value of the numerous contests, old and new, and their many conventions: the high entry and hanging fees, the fuzzy criteria, the confusion of printing quality with design advancement, the weirdly provincial practice of allowing jurors to enter work, the postage-stamp sized reproductions in the annuals.

So it was with some trepidation that I agreed to serve on the jury of this year's ACD 100 Show, though I also felt that it was an honor to be asked, since this particular competition always seemed like one of the respectable ones (and tougher ones to place in, given the limit on the number of works chosen). The invitation was made more enticing by the agreement between the ACD and the show's chairperson, Katherine McCoy, to eliminate the convention of jurying by consensus. I respect the two other jurors immensely, and looked forward to constructing a variation of the juried competition based on this experimental approach. It was going to be fun.

Not long before the jurying, I ran into Michael Beirut in New York, who told me that he had been kidding Kathy McCoy about inviting a jury that "promised to run the gamut from A to B!" Michael's thigh-slapper reminded me of the importance of trying to maintain some sort of objectivity (or at least to avoid acting out my own worst clichés) which of course was at odds with the whole curatorial direction that had been determined for this year's show. I began to suspect that our intention to "fix the format" would prove to be more complicated than we could possibly predict.

No amount of advanced planning quite prepares you for that first glimpse of a football-field sized room full of tables piled with print. I think we jurors quickly recognized that our experiment was about to be tested by two elements that had not been figured into the curatorial model: time (like all juries, we had only seconds to look at each piece, and to analyze whether it fit into our curatorial categories, or not), and selection (unlike curators, who slowly choose works for an exhibition from a theoretically infinite field, we had to choose from a field pre-determined by those who had sent in their work and paid their entry fees, whether they had actually read the published criteria or not).

All of this really did affect the jurying process. As I was inspecting each entry I realized that the work that I *saw* that was the most interesting (to me) was not necessarily in line with my announced criteria. For instance, this was not a big year for "history" (there was less quotation, appropriation, parody, or blatant rip-off). There was a lot of work that appeared to be informed by a knowledge of what has come before, but the issue of "history" just did not seem to jump out of the selections the way we thought it might, given that it was specifically noted in my juror's statement. But a juror's statement, of course, cannot really affect the character of the entries, since most of the entries are created long before the criteria are published. And, by and large, the work that was sent in was not radically different from previous years, reflecting the (vaguely disappointing) state-of-the-art, where the same sorts of projects elicit the same sorts of solutions, over and over again. Perhaps the published criteria did influence a small percentage of the pieces that entrants chose to submit, but I also think that we jurors adjusted our criteria during the process to work with the field of entries that faced us. The result of this friction between the jury's articulated standards and the actual work produced by the entrants is this very interesting hybrid of a show, something like a curated exhibition, but not really.

A note on the jurying process, at the risk of irritating my esteemed colleagues: it didn't quite work out as planned. Despite our different statements, we shared many opinions about the work. Though there were few pieces that all three of us agreed upon, there were lots and lots that two of us liked (in all combinations), but since we had agreed that we would maintain separate selections, we were forced into a sort of flea market, "I-saw-it-first" bartering which, in the end, created artificially larger distinctions between our three sets of choices. Designers whose pieces actually got two votes might be interested to know that; but that would have taken an additional, unforeseen clerical step in the jurying process that was already more complicated by the experiment. I explain this in hope that some future jury continues to tinker with the experiment (and to acknowledge how complicated it is to alter the competition formula).

The issue of time allotted for judging was really crucial to this show because all three of us jurors put such a high value on sense and appropriateness. (I know, from Michael Beirut's witticism, that because all three of us are known for book design and cultural institutional work, that it would be easy to accuse us of impractical artiness. But like myself, Mau and Vermeulen are pragmatists who suspiciously look first for the reason behind everything.) So we felt compelled to read into each entry as best we could. Many good-looking pieces were rejected; some because they were contentless, but more often because, upon closer inspection, content and form were at odds with each other.

Graphic design is at a fascinating moment just now, where influences flow from the fringes into mainstream practice and back in the wake of postmodernism. But the old Achilles heel of graphic design still lingers: style-mongering that is inappropriate, or which just doesn't work, and its depressing corollary, good opportunities for design that go begging. (I don't feel that a banal message necessarily dooms a project to a banal form. I was as impressed by the designers who figured out how to make something visually compelling out of a beer-and-boxing promotion as I was by the designers who produced a visually compelling booklet on human rights activism. In both cases I suspect the designers took an aggressive role in the conceptual development of the works that they produced.) It seems clear that the only way graphic designers are going to continue to justify their existence is by applying the conceptual processes of design with as much intelligence, imagination and grace to all sorts of messages that we, as the audience, will continue to seek out (or endure). But the old issue of appropriateness (and now the newer one of environmental ethics) persists, no matter who the clients are.

In my teaching, I encounter students who think that competitions are so compromised that they should just be abolished. I don't agree with this because despite all of their limitations, they serve as vehicles for the development of an identity for graphic design. After going through this process, I think that the most troublesome aspect of competitions is the narrow range of projects entered, which is still probably influenced more by entry and hanging fees than it is by strategies for jurying. But I was more than happy to contribute to this effort to move the conventions of the competition, and while I don't think we achieved our ideal, I think that it is an improvement: at least this annual will produce a record of how and why each project was selected.

A **Round Table** DISCUSSION WITH LORRAINE WILD, RICK VERMEULEN, AND BRUCE MAU MODERATED BY KATHERINE MCCOY

BM **We saw quite a lot of good work**, it seems to me. In the first cut we selected maybe two hundred pieces. But then on the second look, when trying to find pieces that were consistent throughout, I read more closely and realized that something was missing from much of the work, that it didn't have the quality that I thought it had.

LW One aspect of a piece would be brought to the right level; but then, when you looked more closely, you would find the underpinning of the piece to be wobbly. This of course is the pitfall of most graphic design: the exterior is often very seductive, but it doesn't get you through a second look.

BM I also realized how rarefied a climate I work in, and how so much work in graphic design is not very demanding at all. There is so little work that really reflects the kind of culture that I am interested in, corporate or otherwise.

KM **Do you mean that most of the client messages** brought to designers are not really the kind of material you want to deal with?

BM Yes, because I don't think in terms of client messages.

RV **But you work for the client, don't you?**

BM Yes, but I don't think in those terms. If I take on a project, I take it on in a collaborative sense. I don't think in terms of target audiences or market segments or the kind of terminology that seems to be present in the work that we're seeing.

RV **But doesn't that sound more like art?** I mean, there is a difference.

BM When I went to visit this man in Italy to help him do some work, he asked me "Can you help? Can you tell me how to do this the way that you do it?" I said "I'll tell you how to do this if you tell me how to do art." His response was "There is no difference between what you do and what I do."

KM **This collaborative idea** might not necessarily be dysfunctional. Collaboration could serve the client's communication objectives perfectly well.

BM I think it has to. You must be delivering the product. In marketing terminology, you must be satisfying that client.

LW **Some of what you're saying makes sense** about that ideal of collaboration between the designer and the client. It reminds me of advice that Paul Rand gave students at Yale: *Never talk to anybody below the level of president.* That's where we started in design: a designer would know the entrepreneur president of a company, and they would get together and work as peers (or at least this is the way it's always been described). That's how the seminal work in corporate communications was created. I think it was Tibor Kalman who pointed out that these days an assistant vice president of public relations is working with a representative of a design firm who is not necessarily the person actually at the board producing the work. It makes you wonder what went wrong when you see a good corporate annual report or corporate communications piece. What allowed something good to come out of the current system? Every successful firm reaches a point where they are faced with a choice between growth and control, whether they know it or not. They grow larger, yet seem to ignore the issue of whether they are still producing work as good as when they were smaller, the kind of work which initiated their growth.

KM **Then, occasionally, you do see a firm that just stops** and says, no, wait. And they downscale. I have seen several firms do that in recent years.

LW But you do sacrifice a certain economic success.

KM **Do you always? Is there a model** for this by which economic success isn't sacrificed?

RV I don't think there is.

BM When a firm grows, the quality must be dispersed, because you have to get people who can more or less copy your work to work in a similar manner. Then the quality of their work must be reduced somewhat because it's not a singular gesture, the sort that creates very powerful statements. This is what I'm dealing with in my own situation right now: how to do projects of a bigger scale.

RV If you work on your own, you do everything on the board from start to finish. If you have assistants, you have to think through a project before it actually starts.

KM **That might change your design process** because important thinking often happens while you are in the midst of the execution.

RV What we do a lot is a sort of combination: think beforehand, have the stuff done by someone else, and then finish it or jump in at some point.

KM Rick, you said earlier that you feel the designer should be held responsible for the content of the piece. We saw quite a few pieces that dealt with environmental issues and, in a few cases, social issues. What did you think about that work, and why did you reject some of it?

RV **It's very much a fashion.** A lot of firms get into environmental issues and recycled paper, and all that stuff to look good – to be nice, to do what

American Center for Design FOURTEENTH ANNUAL 100 SHOW

8

9

Fourteenth Annual 100 Show
American Center for Design
Book cover, text and divider pages
Designer/illustrator: Mark D. Sylvester
Design company: Point/Cranbrook
Academy of Art
Client: American Center for Design
USA, 1991

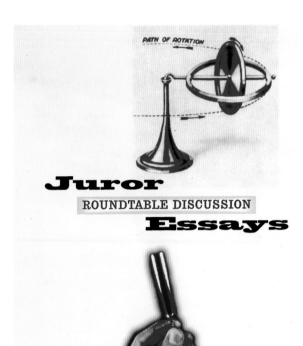

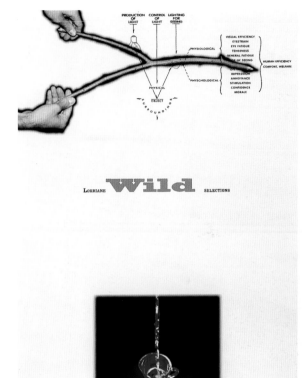

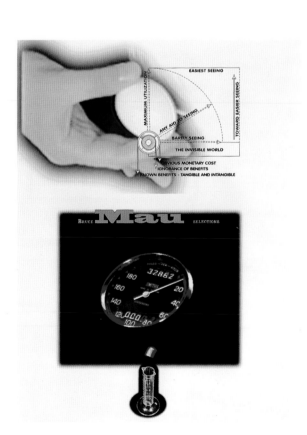

THE
EYE mind
MINNEAPOLIS
COLLEGE
of
ART
+
DESIGN

The Minneapolis College of
Art + Design 1991-1993
Prospectus cover
Designer: P. Scott Makela
Design company: P. Scott Makela Words +
Pictures for Business + Culture
Client: Minneapolis College of Art and Design
USA, 1991

Do Nothing
Visual essay from the catalogue
Rethinking Design
Designer: P. Scott Makela
Catalogue designer: Michael Bierut,
Pentagram
Client: Mohawk Paper
USA, 1992

SINCE OBJECTS SHOW UP BETTER IN PICTURES THERE HAS ALWAYS BEEN AN EMPHASIS ON THINGS DESIGNERS MAKE

DO

TUCKER VIEMEISTER

P. SCOTT MAKELA

BY
SCOTT MAKELA AND BENOIT BARBIER

EVEN WHEN WE TALK ABOUT THE NON-PHYSICAL ASPECTS OF DESIGN IT IS USUALLY IN TERMS OF SYSTEMS (THE WAY THE GROUPS OF PRODUCTS INTERACT) OR THE INTERFACE (THE DYNAMIC CONNECTION BETWEEN US AND THE PRODUCT OR SPACE (THE VOLUME FORMED BETWEEN THE OBJECTS). BUT AS I WALK THROUGH THE WINTER RAIN, I AM THINKING ABOUT ANOTHER POWERFUL INVISIBLE FORM OF DESIGN - DOING NOTHING.

NOTHING.

SLEEP

Dormancy is an important part of any life cycle - sleep is the pause that refreshes. Autumn and winter rejuvenate plants and animals. Meditation helps us refocus our soul. Computers frozen to absolute zero compute faster.

Tokyo Salamander:
American Dream Diary 1989
Spreads from an artist's book
Designer: Vaughan Oliver
Design company: v23
Artist: Shinro Ohtake
Client: Shinro Ohtake/Kyoto Shoin
Great Britain, 1993

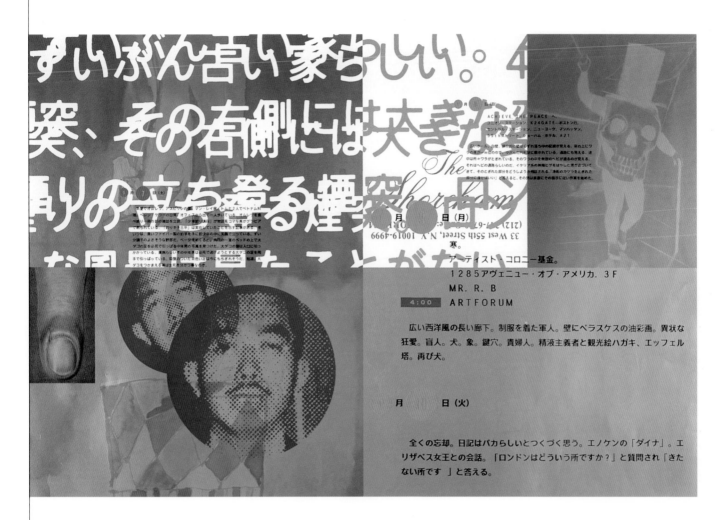

Lyceum Fellowship
Competition posters
Designers: Nancy Skolos, Thomas Wedell
Design company: Skolos/Wedell
Photographer: Thomas Wedell
Client: Lyceum Fellowship Committee
USA, 1992, 1993

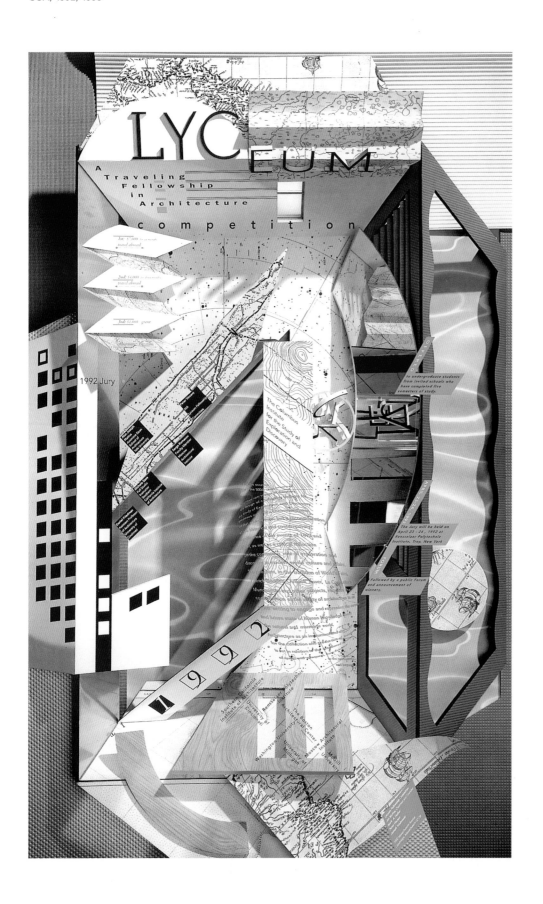

Lyceum Fellowship
Competition posters
Designers: Nancy Skolos, Thomas Wedell
Design company: Skolos/Wedell
Photographer: Thomas Wedell
Client: Lyceum Fellowship Committee
USA, 1992, 1993

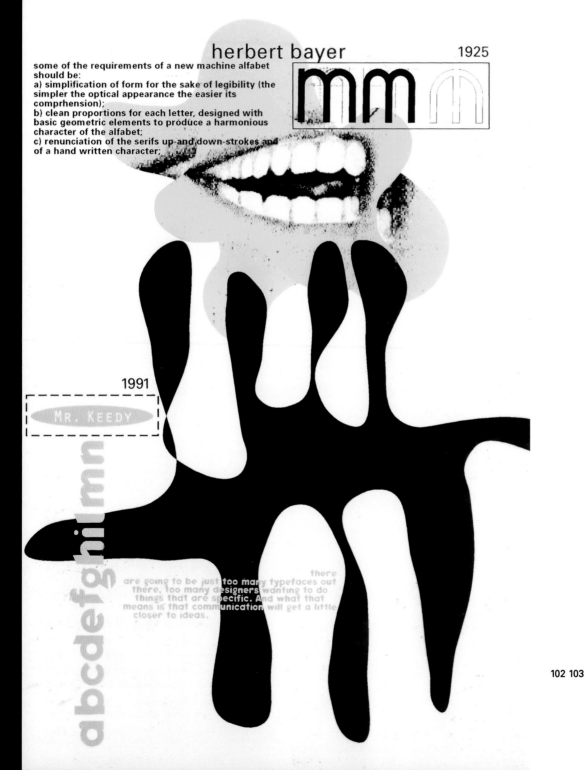

herbert bayer 1925

some of the requirements of a new machine alfabet
should be:
a) simplification of form for the sake of legibility (the
simpler the optical appearance the easier its
comprhension);
b) clean proportions for each letter, designed with
basic geometric elements to produce a harmonious
character of the alfabet;
c) renunciation of the serifs up-and-down-strokes and
of a hand written character;

1991

MR. KEEDY

abcdefghijklmn

there
are going to be just too many typefaces out
there, too many designers wanting to do
things that are specific. And what that
means is that communication will get a little
closer to ideas.

102 103

Herbert Bayer/Jeff Keedy Type History
Poster
Designer: Joan Dobkin
Self-published, Cranbrook Academy of Art
USA, 1991

GAM (Graphic Arts Message)
Poster
Designer: Neville Brody
Design company: Neville Brody Studio
Client: Too Corporation
Great Britain, 1992

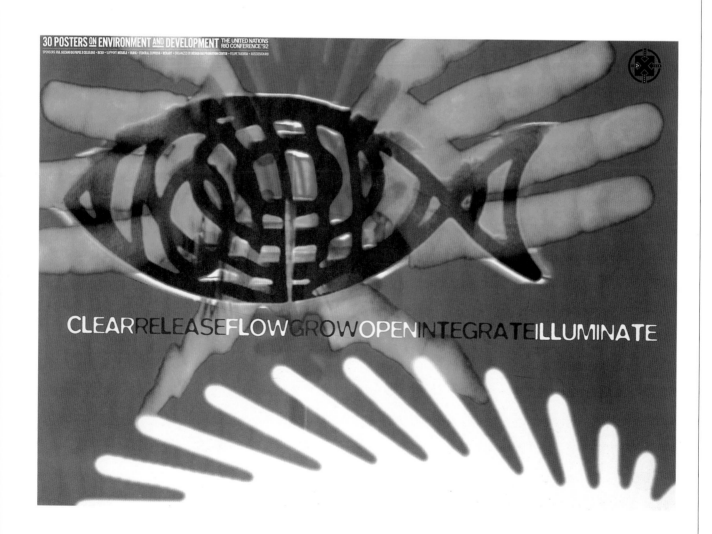

Rio Festival
Poster
Designer: Neville Brody
Design company: Neville Brody Studio
Client: Design Rio, Brazil
Great Britain, 1992

Fuse
Promotional posters for interactive
typeface magazine
Designer: Neville Brody
Design company: Neville Brody Studio
Client: FontShop International
Great Britain, 1992, 1993

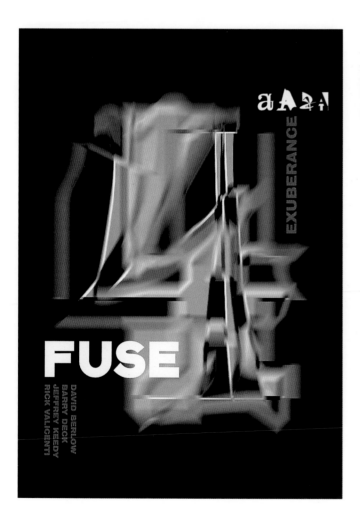

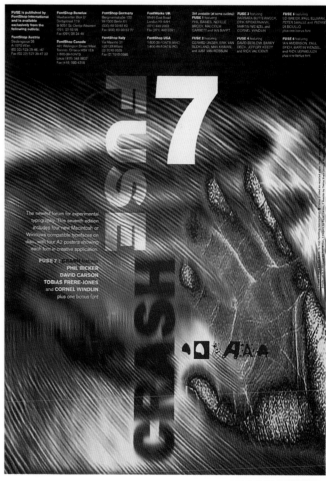

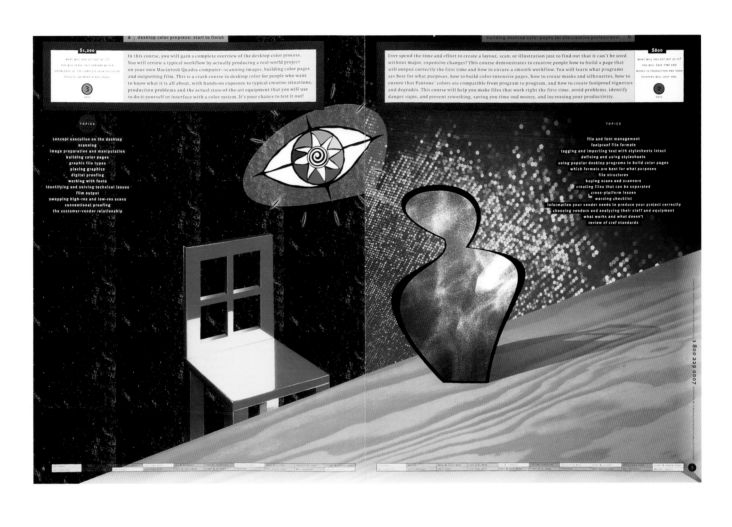

$1,200

WHAT WILL YOU GET OUT OF IT? YOU WILL LEAVE THIS SEMINAR WITH A KNOWLEDGE OF THE COMPLETE DESKTOP COLOR PROCESS, NO MORE BLACK HOLES.

3 DAYS

In this course, you will gain a complete overview of the desktop color process. You will review a typical workflow by actually producing a real-world project on your own Macintosh Quadra computer—scanning images, building color pages and outputting film. This is a crash course in desktop color for people who want to know what it is all about, with hands-on exposure to typical creative situations, production problems and the actual state-of-the-art equipment that you will use to do-it-yourself or interface with a color system. It's your chance to test it out!

Ever spend the time and effort to create a layout, scan, or illustration just to find out that it can't be used without major, expensive changes? This course demonstrates to creative people how to build a page that will output correctly the first time and how to ensure a smooth workflow. You will learn what programs are best for what purposes, how to build color-intensive pages, how to create masks and silhouettes, how to ensure that Pantone° colors are compatible from program to program, and how to create foolproof vignettes and degradés. This course will help you make files that work right the first time, avoid problems, identify danger signs, and prevent reworking, saving you time and money, and increasing your productivity.

$800

WHAT WILL YOU GET OUT OF IT? YOU WILL SAVE TIME AND MONEY IN PRODUCTION AND YOUR PRINTERS WILL LOVE YOU.

2 DAYS

TOPICS

concept execution on the desktop
scanning
image preparation and manipulation
building color pages
graphic file types
placing graphics
digital proofing
working with fonts
identifying and solving technical issues
film output
swapping high-res and low-res scans
conventional proofing
the customer-vendor relationship

TOPICS

file and font management
foolproof file formats
tagging and importing text with stylesheets intact
defining and using stylesheets
using popular desktop programs to build color pages
which formats are best for what purposes
file structures
buying scans and scanners
creating files that can be separated
cross-platform issues
warning checklist
information your vendor needs to produce your project correctly
choosing vendors and analyzing their staff and equipment
what works and what doesn't
review of cref standards

1 800 239 0007

Add a Little Magic
Brochure spreads
Designer: Rick Valicenti
Typographers: Rick Valicenti, Richard Weaver, Tracy Taylor
Design company: Thirst
Photographers: Corinne Pfister, Michael Pappas
Digital imaging: Tony Klassen, Mark Rattin
Client: The Color Center
USA, 1992

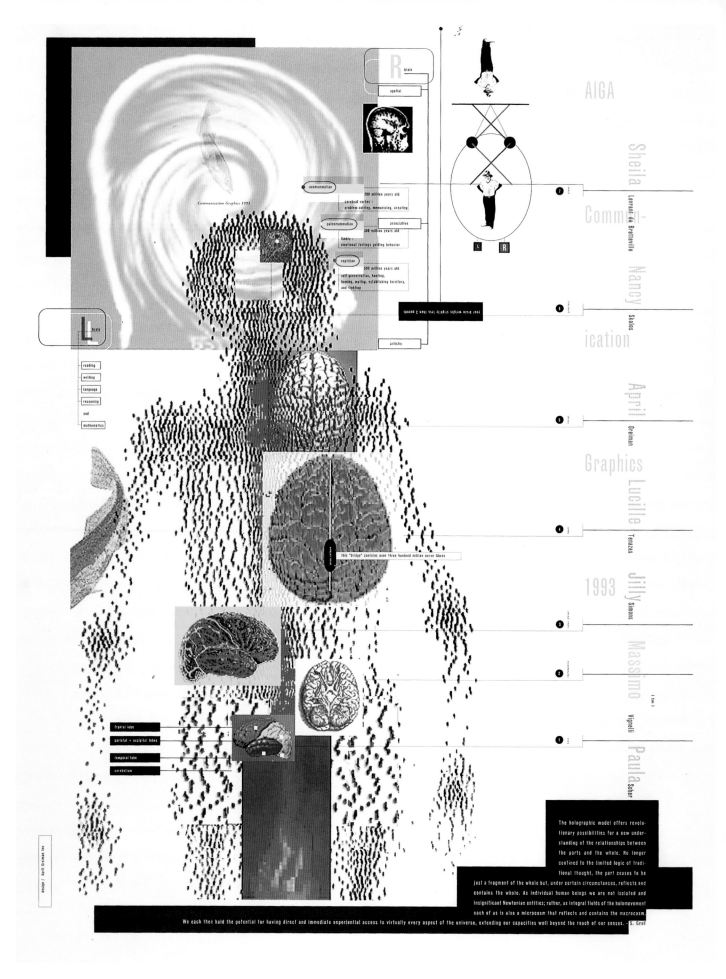

AIGA Communication Graphics 1993
Competition poster
Designer: April Greiman
Associate designer: Sean Adams
Design company: April Greiman Inc.
Client: American Institute of Graphic Arts
USA, 1992

Live-Able Benign Architecture
Poster
Designer/illustrator: Mark D. Sylvester
Design company: Point
Self-published, Cranbrook Academy of Art
USA, 1991

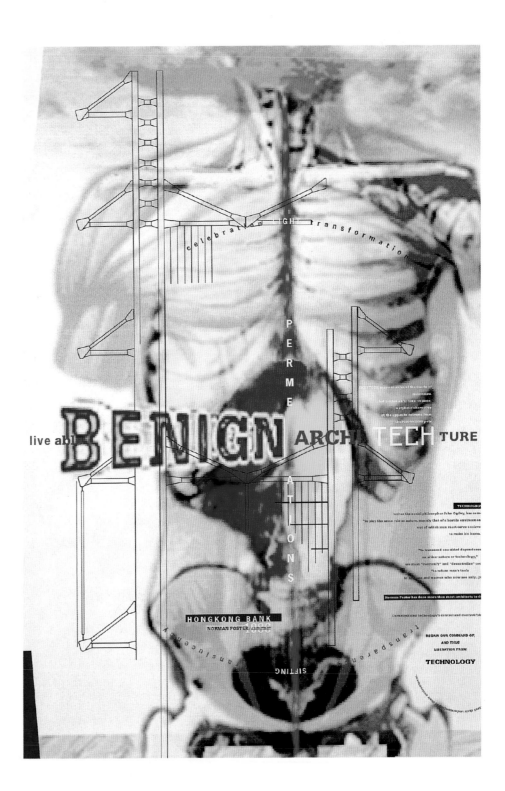

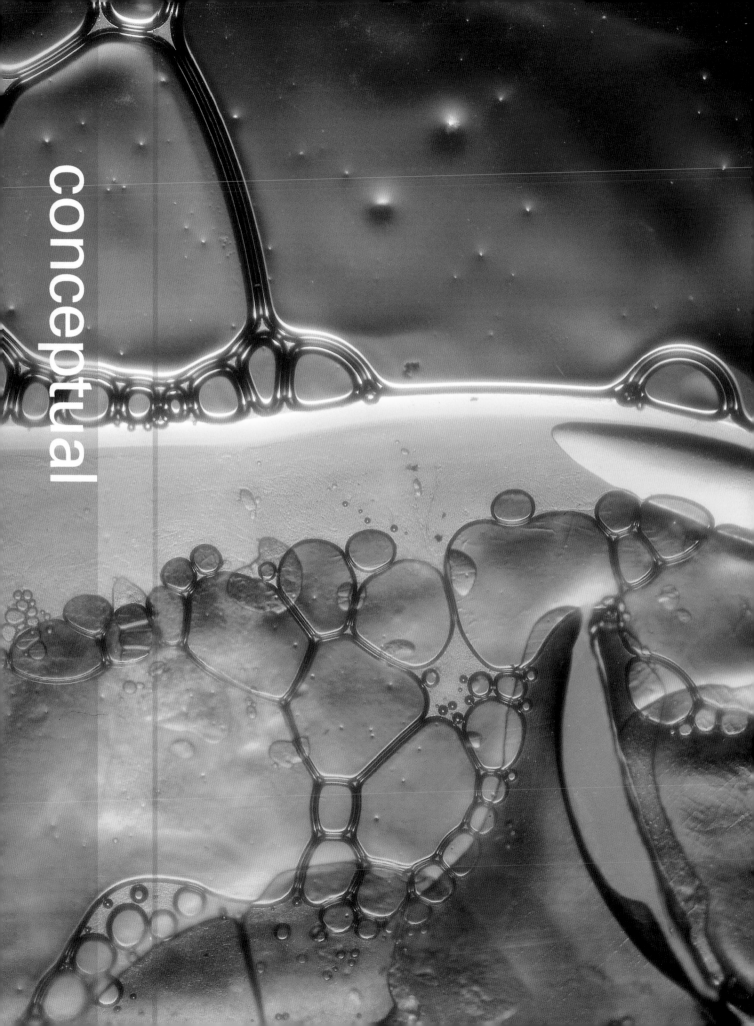

conceptual

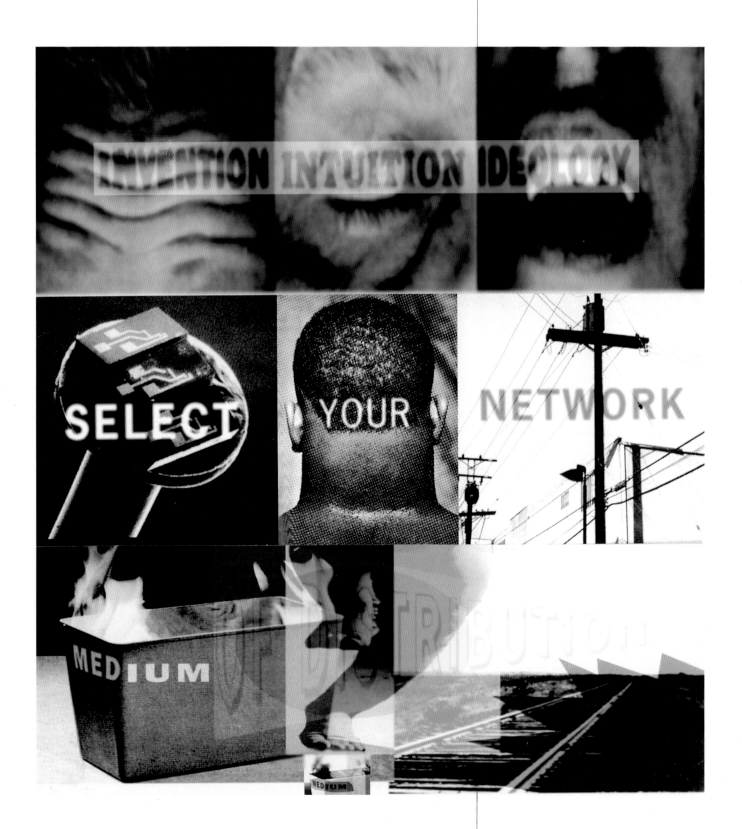

Select Your Network
Poster
Designer: P. Scott Makela
Self-published, Cranbrook Academy of Art
USA, 1990

Self-promotional advertisement
Designers: Ian Cartlidge, Adam Levene,
Sean Perkins, Yumi Matote, Simon Browning
Design company: Cartlidge Levene
Photographer: Peter Robathan
Great Britain, 1991

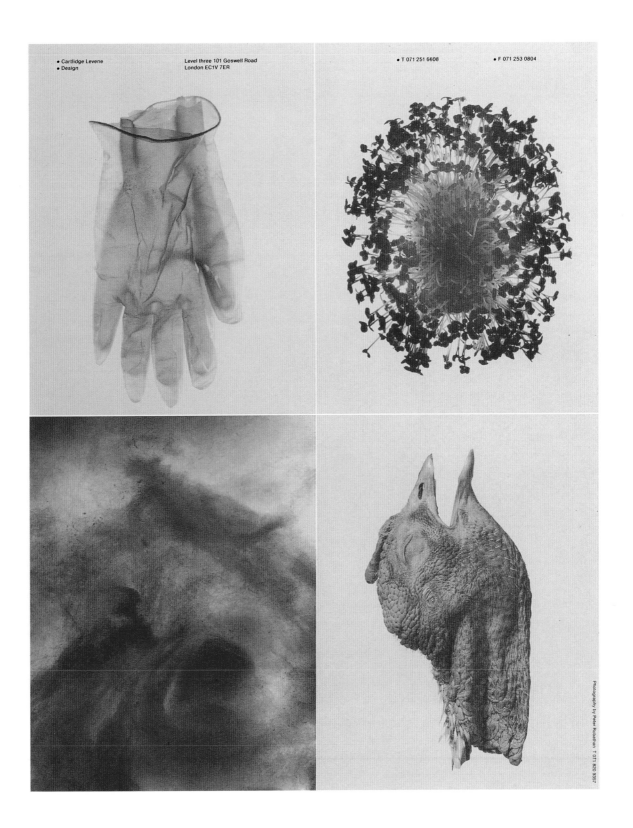

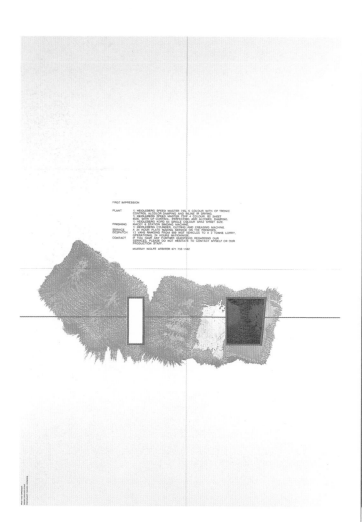

FIRST IMPRESSION

PLANT   1) HEIDELBERG SPEED MASTER 72S, 6 COLOUR WITH CP TRONIC
           CONTROL, ALCOLOR DAMPING AND INLINE IR DRYING.
           1) HEIDELBERG SPEED MASTER 72VP 4 COLOUR, B2 SHEET
           SIZE, WITH CP CONTROL, PERFECTING AND ALCOMIL DAMPING.
           1) HEIDELBERG KORD 64 SINGLE COLOUR SRA2 SHEET SIZE.
FINISHING MACEY 8 STATION BINDING MACHINE.
           1) HEIDELBERG CYLINDER, CUTTING AND CREASING MACHINE.
SERVICE   A 24 HOUR PLATE MAKING SERVICE ON THE PREMISES.
DESPATCH   13 VANS RANGING FROM 900 WGT VEHICLES TO A 3 TONNE LORRY.
           OPERATIONAL 24 HOURS NATIONWIDE.
CONTACT   IF YOU HAVE ANY FURTHER QUESTIONS REGARDING OUR
           SERVICES, PLEASE DO NOT HESITATE TO CONTACT MYSELF OR OUR
           PRODUCTION STAFF.

           MURRAY WOLFE ARBITER 071 733 1182

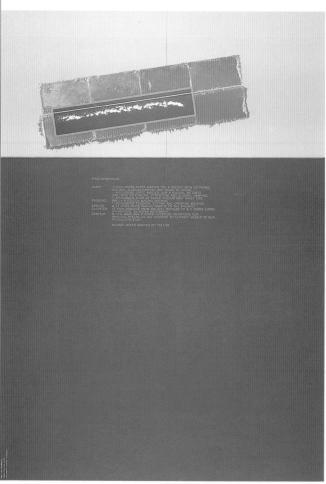

FIRST IMPRESSION

PLANT   1) HEIDELBERG SPEED MASTER 72S, 6 COLOUR WITH CP TRONIC
           CONTROL, ALCOLOR DAMPING AND INLINE IR DRYING.
           1) HEIDELBERG SPEED MASTER 72VP 4 COLOUR, B2 SHEET
           SIZE, WITH CP CONTROL, PERFECTING AND ALCOMIL DAMPING.
           1) HEIDELBERG KORD 64 SINGLE COLOUR SRA2 SHEET SIZE.
FINISHING MACEY 8 STATION BINDING MACHINE.
           1) HEIDELBERG CYLINDER, CUTTING AND CREASING MACHINE.
SERVICE   A 24 HOUR PLATE MAKING SERVICE ON THE PREMISES.
DESPATCH   13 VANS RANGING FROM 900 WGT VEHICLES TO A 3 TONNE LORRY.
           OPERATIONAL 24 HOURS NATIONWIDE.
CONTACT   IF YOU HAVE ANY FURTHER QUESTIONS REGARDING OUR
           SERVICES, PLEASE DO NOT HESITATE TO CONTACT MYSELF OR OUR
           PRODUCTION STAFF.

           MURRAY WOLFE ARBITER 071 733 1182

Promotional posters
Designer: Simon Browning
Design company: Cartlidge Levene
Photographer: Richard J. Burbridge
Client: First Impression Printers
Great Britain, 1991

Poster for a Geometrician
Designer: Elliott Peter Earls
Self-published, Cranbrook Academy of Art
USA, 1991

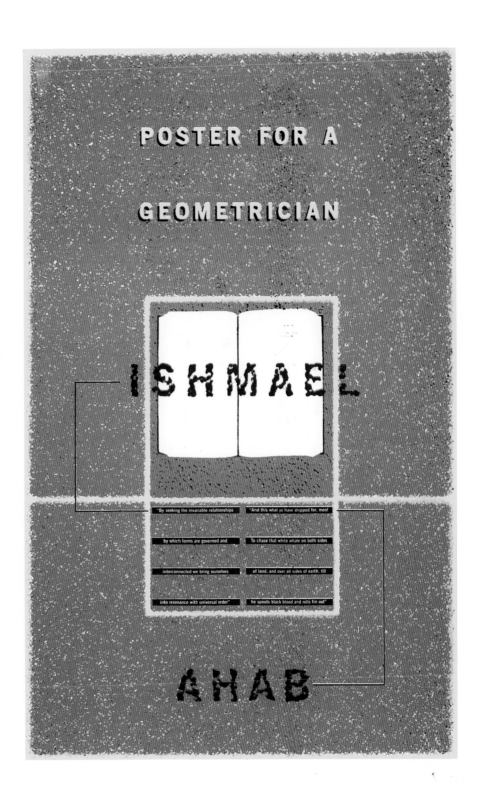

The Creative Community:
Working in Europe
Conference poster
Designers: Simon Browning, Yumi Matote
Design company: Cartlidge Levene
Photographer: Tomoko Yoneda
Client: Design Museum, London
Great Britain, 1992

Conference mailer
Designer: Cornel Windlin
Photographer: Istvan Balogh
Client: Museum für Gestaltung, Zurich
Great Britain, 1993

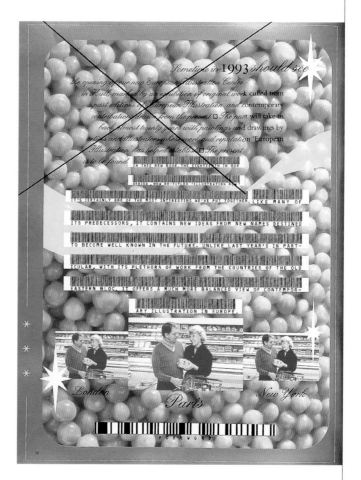

Illustration Now
Book foreword page and divider pages
Designer: Jonathan Barnbrook
Client: Booth-Clibborn Editions
Great Britain, 1993

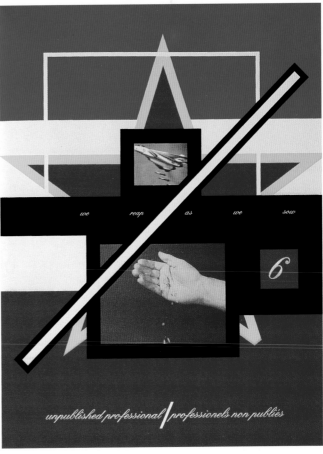

NEW YORK CITY

CARTLIDGE LEVENE 071 251 6608   RICHARD J BURBRIDGE 071 739 5786   PRECISE LITHO 071 253 588

New York City
Self-promotional advertisement
Designers: Simon Browning,
Sean Perkins, Yumi Matote
Design company: Cartlidge Levene
Photographer: Richard J. Burbridge
Great Britain, 1992

GERALD VAN DER KAAP

hover
hover

A MANUAL
STEDELIJK MUSEUM
AMSTERDAM

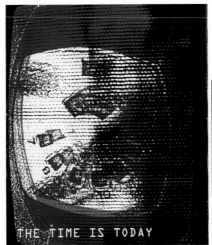

THE TIME IS TODAY

preFACE

welcome to the hover house

QA

Interview by Dorine Mignot

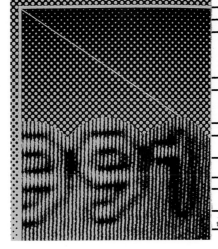

reflex ; ?	!; generate
consumer activism	so what
sky-dive; fall (g)	hover hover (low-g/zero-g)
DON'T	**DO**
weefgetouw	zweefgetouw
the 80's	the 90's
60's (zero)	(digital zero) 10's
i = information E.T.	√-1 = i (as in happY) E.V. (en ville)
true	yes, negative
deconstructing lies...............	constructing lies........ (using carnivalesque strategies
mirrors	windows (0.1 portholes)
(...)	the adulterated new
everyday sign systems transformed into new meaning	new sign systems. from zero.

Architect's promotional brochure/poster
Designers: Morag Myerscough,
Jane Chipchase
Design company: Myerscough Chipchase
Client: Iain MacDonald, Arquitectura
Great Britain, 1992

Total Hoverty
Exhibition flyer/poster
Designers: Armand Mevis, Linda van Deursen
Design company: Mevis & van Deursen
Client: Gerald van der Kaap
The Netherlands, 1992

ARQUITECTURA'S CORE DESIGN TEAM OF ARCHITECTS, ENGINEERS AND DESIGNERS HAS BEEN ASSEMBLED TO MEET THE CURRENT REVOLUTION IN BUSINESS AND ESPECIALLY IN BUILDING MATERIALS. MASTERPLANNING: ROYAL VICTORIA DOCKS LONDON, WARSAW FINANCIAL CENTRE, PORT EAST DOCKLANDS, CENTRAL RIMINI, CENTRAL BUSINESS DISTRICT MILTON KEYNES, M8 EAST FLANK/M74 EXTENSION. ARCHITECTURE: RETAIL SHOWROOMS IN LONDON MILAN AMSTERDAM MUNICH, BANKS IN ITALY AND PORTUGAL, RESIDENCES IN ITALY AND UK PAVILIONS FOR EXPO 92 SEVILLE, IT/R+D FACILITIES IN UK AND GERMANY, RESTAURANTS AND BARS IN UK ITALY HOLLAND AND RUSSIA. SPECIAL PROJECTS: TELEVISION SET DESIGN, PRODUCT DESIGN, FURNITURE DESIGN AND DESIGN RESEARCH WE BELIEVE THAT CLEAR AND PRECISE COMMUNICATION IS AN ESSENTIAL ELEMENT OF THE PROJECT PROCESS. WE THEREFORE DELIVER OUR IDEAS IN A WIDE RANGE OF MIXED MEDIA.

THE MOST CRITICAL ASPECT OF CREATING A NEW ENVIRONMENT IS NOT SO MUCH TO SATISFY A SET OF ALREADY DEFINED NEEDS BUT TO ARRIVE AT A NEW AND UNIQUE DEFINITION.
ARQUITECTURA'S PURPOSE IS TO PROVIDE A FRESH INTERFACE BETWEEN COMMERCIAL ENTERPRISE AND DESIGN CULTURE "AS WE ENTER AN ERA WHEREIN ARCHITECTURE FORMS ONE LAYER OF A CODA IN WHICH THE HIGHLY ARTI-FICIAL OVERLAPS WITH THE NATURAL". (Domus)
ARQUITECTURA RECOGNISE THAT "THE VALUE OF ANY COOPERATIVE PARTNERSHIP FOR BOTH SIDES, LIES PRECISELY IN THE DIFFERENCES OF VIEWPOINT AND BACKGROUND WHICH EACH BRINGS TO THE RELATIONSHIP". (Domus)
OUR ARCHITECTURE FOR INDIVIDUAL AND CORPORATE CLIENTS IS CREATED BY A CORE TEAM OF ARCHITECTS DRAWN FROM LINKED STUDIOS IN LONDON, MILAN AND TOKYO.

NO PREDICTABLE RESULTS.

WHEN I THINK OF IAIN MACDONALD, I PICTURE A WORLD WHERE PEOPLE (BODY AND SOUL), BUILD-INGS, ROOMS AND THINGS ARE ENDOWED WITH THE UTMOST ORIGINALITY. FRESH FORMS, COLOURS AND ATTITUDES MAKE IAIN'S WORLD CHEERFUL, FUTURE, INTELLIGENT AND RICH IN MODERN HUMANITY.

Alessandro Mendini
ARCHITECT, MILAN.

3D/AE (EXHIBITION MODEL)

HOW

TOTAL HOVERTY IS BASED ON THE **BRAIN 5.1** INFORMATION SYSTEM THAT CONTROLS THE INSTALLATION ENVIRONMENT. THERE ARE AN ALMOST UNLIMITED VARIETY OF EXHIBITIONS POSSIBLE THROUGH THE SELECTION AND OUTPUT OF **BRAIN 5.1**. A NEWLY DEVELOPED INTERFACE, THE **CHILL TERMINAL 3.2**, WILL PROVIDE INSTANT MYSTICAL PEAK-EXPERIENCE.

5.1

TOTAL HOVERTY

WHAT

BRAIN 5.1 (TEST) PHOTOSOFT (35MM SLIDES) > SCREENS (CAVE)

BRAIN 5.1 (WORDS) VIDEOSOFT (VHS) > SCREENS (CAVE)

びしょ濡れ血管
わたしは 流れる血管

E1 (INITIATION). YO. HELLO. HOW ARE YOU. GOODBYE. I GO. I WANT MY CLOTHES WASHED. I WANT THIS MENDED. A KNIFE. I CUT THE BOOK. ETERNAL DIAMOND. GO... E2 (HELL)...HELL. I WANT ANOTHER TABLE. PLEASE, I WANT A FACE MASSAGE. THIS IS NOT FRESH. (I NEED A FIX CAUSE I'M GOING DOWN. THE FALSE CHARACTER THAT FOLLOWS YOU AROUND.*) I'LL PRAY FOR RAIN, FAIR WEATHER, FOR HELL ... E 3 (HOVERPOINT)....OF COURSE. I UNDERSTAND. I KNOW EXACTLY WHAT YOU MEAN. ROOT OUT. PULL DOWN. DESTROY. LOOK AT THE SKY. GO WITH THE FLOW. WALK ON. YOUR LIFE. EARN IT. SPEND IT. SAVE IT. SPILL IT. WHERE IT CAN DO SOME GOOD. O.K. YES, NEGATIVE.... E 4 (HEAVEN) ....HEY YOU. I SAW YOU. BODY MYSTIC. THANKS. HERE SHE COMES. SIR. SIRE. SYRINGE. SYRINX. SISTER. SECRET NIGHT. DIE INTO ME. YOU. YO... T'

PATTERN: E1 (INITIATION) > E2 (HELL) > E3 (HOVERPOINT) > E4 (HEAVEN) > REPEAT

Heaven and hell are one word

BRAIN 5.1 (TOTAL HOVERTY) AUDIOSOFT (DAT) HEADSETS

Our method is techno. Our aim is total hoverty.

BRAIN 5.1 (SIRENS) AUDIOSOFT (DAT) > P.A. SYSTEM

BRAIN 5.1 (BODY SONIC) AUDIOSOFT (DAT) > BODY SONIC OUTPUT

DON'T a i THINK &

BRAIN 5.1 (TYPE ZERO) VIDEOSOFT (VHS) > CHILL TERMINAL

BRAIN 5.1 (TYPE ONE) VIDEOSOFT (VHS) > CHILL TERMINAL

b r

*) Adult Cave Life

CHILL TERMINAL 3.2
Interface for Brain 5.1
No other drugs required.

FOR ADULT CAVE LIFE.
All senses operative.
Destination: total hoverty.

PPPP Symposium
Poster
Designers: Armand Mevis, Linda van Deursen
Design company: Mevis & van Deursen
Client: Jan van Eyck Academy, Maastricht
The Netherlands, 1992

In the Spirit of Fluxus
Exhibition catalogue cover and spreads
Designers: Laurie Haycock Makela,
Mark Nelson
Client: Walker Art Center, Minneapolis
USA, 1992

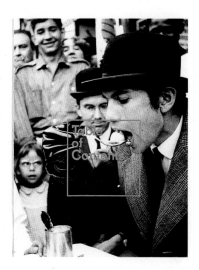

HOLIDAY

above
Slowly, steadily

the bright sky
deepened

ACTION!

Break Break Break

Break time.

HOLIDAY COCKTAIL LOUNGE

Mr. Emerson
sits in his leather chair.
TV on; Cheese Nachos
News time, open.
last hours' report
retreated
repeated.

Strange compulsion within Compelled towards horrific
gruesome items

Make more coffee.

Back in chair,
tastes sour —
down the sink, rancid milk.

Sick,
anxious
feeling
What's the worry?
No one knows his location.
Do they?
Do they?

Little wedge
of doubt
gets a clout.
Make the first move.
Out.

"The new American poetry as typified by the SF Renaissance (which means Ginsberg, me, Rexroth, Ferlinghetti, McClure, Corso, Gary Snyder, Philip Lamantia, Philip Whalen, I guess) is a kind of new-old Zen Lunacy poetry, writing whatever comes into your head as it comes, poetry returned to its origin, in the bardic child, truly ORAL as Ferling said, instead of gray faced Academic quibbling. Poetry & prose had for long time fallen into the false hands of the false. These new pure poets confess forth for the sheer joy of confession. They are CHILDREN! They are also childlike graybeard Homers singing in the street. They SING, they SWING. It is diametrically opposed to the Eliot shot, who so distinctly advises his dreary negative rules like the objective correlative, etc. which is just a lot of constipation and ultimately emasculation of the pure masculine urge to freely sing. In spite of the dry rules he set down his poetry is itself sublime. I could write forever on the difference between the two kinds of poetry of a new Holy Lunacy like that of ancient times (Li Po, Hanshan, Tom O Bedlam, Kit Smart, Blake) yet it also has that mental discipline typified by the haiku (Basho, Buson), that is, the discipline of pointing out things directly, purely, concretely, no abstractions or explanations, wham wham the true blue song of man.
Jack Kerouac – The Origins of Joy in Poetry

"The word of course is one of the most powerful instruments of control... Now if you start cutting these up and rearranging them you are breaking down the control system"

"Burroughs maintains that the only relative, etc. . . alter the playback . . . that are used by others (personally and politically) to control . . . is through 'counterrecording' and playback,' a procedure of repetition, manipulation and purposeful distortion used as a tool of analysis and aggression."

Nude Language
Poster
Designer/photographer: Elliott Peter Earls
Self-published, Cranbrook Academy of Art
USA, 1992

Image as Weapon
Poster/mailer
Designer: P. Scott Makela
Design company: P. Scott Makela Words +
Pictures for Business + Culture
Client: Walker Art Center, Minneapolis
USA, 1992

ARTIFICIAL

NATURE

Artificial Nature
Exhibition catalogue cover and spreads
Designer: Dan Friedman
Editors: Jeffrey Deitch, Dan Friedman
Client: Deste Foundation
for Contemporary Art, Athens
USA, 1990

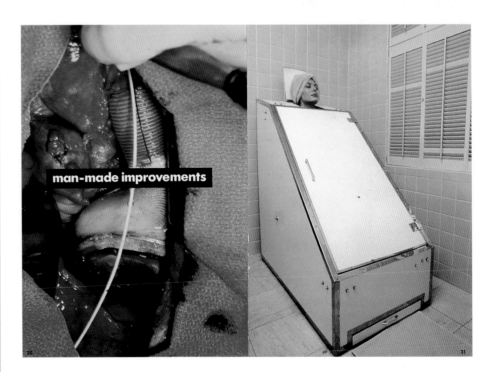

spiritualizing it

infusing it with emotion

42

43

*more and more something that we are re-creating
ourselves.* From the greenhouse effect that could
change our climate, to the green revolution that
has spawned supercharged strains of grains and
vegetables, nature is being reconstituted. For today's
average city dweller, nature is more often than not
something to be experienced on television, or on a
Club Med vacation. There are still many people who
earn their living from the land and the sea, and for
whom nature is very real. For the rest of us, however,
nature is an increasingly artificial experience.

Art and nature have been inextricably linked ever
since the cave paintings of Lascaux. *Nature has
traditionally been the ultimate inspiration and
challenge for the artist who, depending on his or
her orientation, sought to imitate it, improve upon it,
or interpret it.* Our conception of nature has often
been derived, in fact, from the vision of artists. Our
sense of what nature is has been shaped and
reshaped by artists of successive generations, such
as Leone Battista Alberti, Claude Lorrain, J.M.W.
Turner, and the Impressionists. Not only have artists
studied nature for centuries, they have also looked to
it for the revelation of basic truths. An immersion in

nature and its forms gave artists, scientists, and phi-
losophers a deeper picture of reality.

An artist can still pack a portable easel and hike into
the mountains to sketch a small section of wilderness,
but a truly contemporary artist might be better
advised to seek truth in nature in a strip mine or in
the visitors' center of a game preserve. To immerse
oneself in nature today is to uncover layers of chaotic
exploitation and man-made "improvements."
*Genuine nature may now be more artificial
than natural.*

From the genetic reconstitution of human beings, to
the growth of a kind of worldwide suburbia, we are
slowly but steadily replacing what we knew to be
nature with a new kind of artificial nature. It is not
just that an average person can easily go through
years of life breathing air-conditioned air, playing
football on Astroturf, and the like, but that a new
model of reality is replacing our old sense of the natural order. The jungle ride at Disney World may in fact
be more real to most people than the real jungle in
the Amazon. Artificially colored and genetically
enhanced oranges are perceived to look and taste

Artificial Nature
Exhibition catalogue spreads
Designer: Dan Friedman
Editors: Jeffrey Deitch, Dan Friedman
Client: Deste Foundation
for Contemporary Art, Athens
USA, 1990

Post
HUMAN

Post Human
Exhibition catalogue cover and spreads
Designer: Dan Friedman
Picture editors: Jeffrey Deitch, Dan Friedman
Client: Deste Foundation
for Contemporary Art, Athens
USA, 1992

The extraordinary self-transformation

of Ivana Trump is an example of this shuffling of

reality and

fantasy

into a reassembled fictional personality.

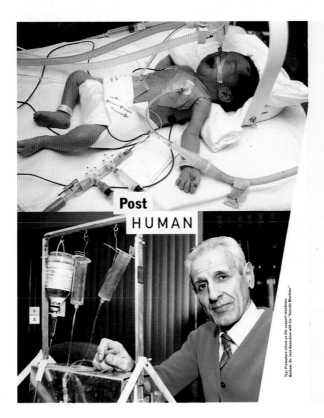

Post HUMAN

Top: Premature infant on life-support machines
Bottom: Dr. Jack Kevorkian with his "Suicide Machine"

On most people's beauty scale, Stacey Stetler would be a 10. A blond, blue-eyed, 5-foot-11 New York model, she has confidently sashayed down the runway for Yves Saint Laurent in Paris and has graced the covers of fashion magazines. But until recently, when Ms. Stetler looked in the mirror she saw less perfection and more flaws. "I was flat-chested," Ms. Stetler said. "You couldn't tell if I was coming or going. My back protruded almost as much as my front.". . .Ms. Stetler enhanced her boyish figure by having breast implants. She is not alone.
The New York Times, 6 February 1992, front page

Stories about breast implants, crash diets, and mood drugs have moved from the health and beauty page to the front page. The public has been galvanized by explosive testimony about sexual harassment and by the sensational rape trials of public figures. Questions about the new boundaries of appropriate interpersonal behavior are attracting unprecedented interest. There is a growing sense that we should take control over our bodies and our social circumstances rather than just accepting what we inherited.

Social and scientific trends are converging to shape a new conception of the self, a new construction of what it means to be a human being. The matter-of-fact acceptance of one's "natural" looks and one's "natural" personality is being replaced by a growing sense that it is normal to reinvent oneself. The Freudian model of the "psychological person" is dissolving into a new model that encourages individuals to dispense with the anguished analysis of how subconscious childhood experiences molded their behavior. There is a new sense that one can simply construct the new self that one wants, freed from the constraints of one's past and one's inherited genetic code.

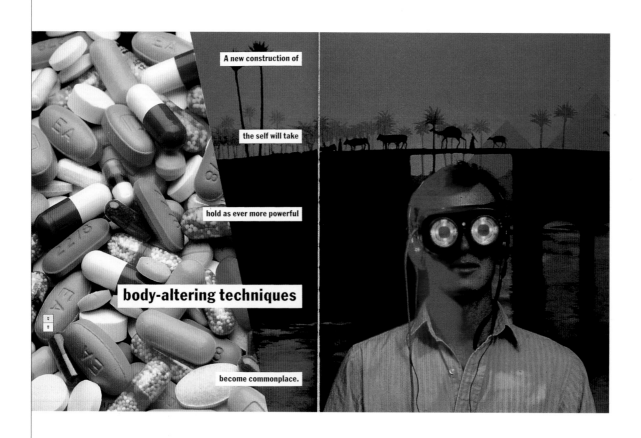

A new construction of

the self will take

hold as ever more powerful

body-altering techniques

become commonplace.

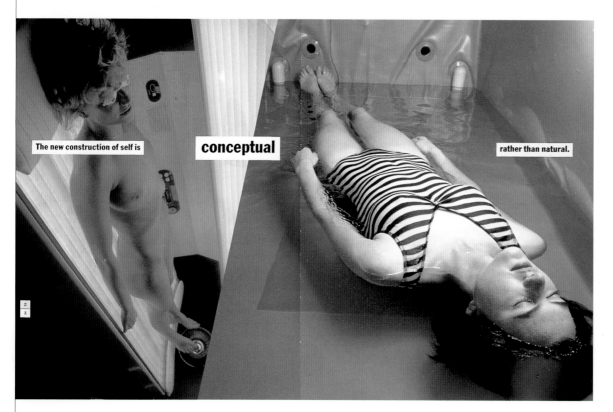

The new construction of self is **conceptual** rather than natural.

Post Human
Exhibition catalogue spreads
Designer: Dan Friedman
Picture editors: Jeffrey Deitch, Dan Friedman
Client: Deste Foundation
for Contemporary Art, Athens
USA, 1992

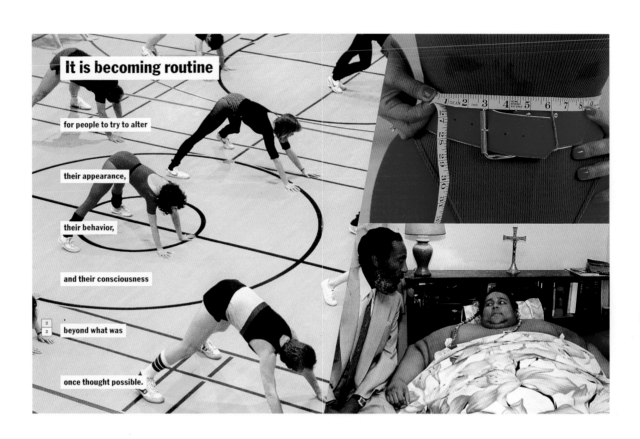

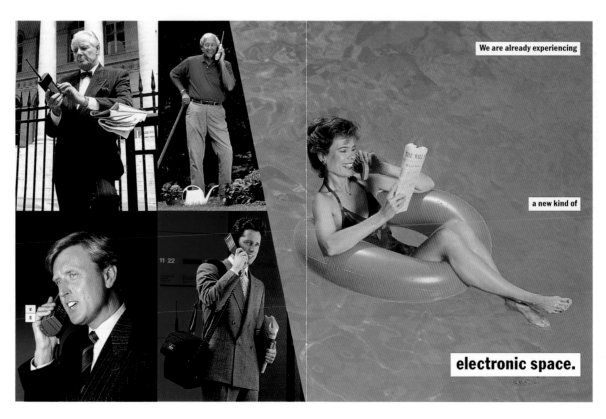

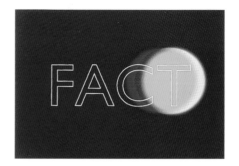

140 141

HIV/AIDS awareness cards
Designers: Alan Aboud, Sandro Sodano
Design company: Aboud-Sodano
Photographer: Sandro Sodano
Client: The Terrence Higgins Trust
Great Britain, 1992

INSPIRAL CARPETS

THIS IS HOW IT FEELS: THE SINGLE

"WHEN IT COMES TO POP PROWESS THEY REMAIN IN A TOTALLY *DIFFERENT* STRATOSPHERE"

SOUNDS

Elektra

BRAND NUBIAN

"SKILLS! SKILLS! SKILLS!

GRAND PUBA A CLEVER RHYMER SINCE THE

MASTERS OF CEREMONY DAYS.

GIVE HIM AND HIS CREW PROPS, NOW!"

CHUCK D PUBLIC ENEMY

SLOW DOWN: THE SINGLE

RUSH ARTIST MANAGEMENT

Elektra

Game Over.

This Was Tomorrow.

Yohji Yamamoto Autumn/Winter 91/92
Press advertising campaign
Art director: Peter Saville
Designers: Stephen Wolstenholme,
Brett Wickens
Design company: Pentagram
Photographer: photolibrary
Client: Yohji Yamamoto
Great Britain, 1991

Republic
Album cover
Art director: Peter Saville
Designer: Brett Wickens
Design company: Pentagram
Photographer: photolibrary
Client: CentreDate/London Records
Great Britain, 1993

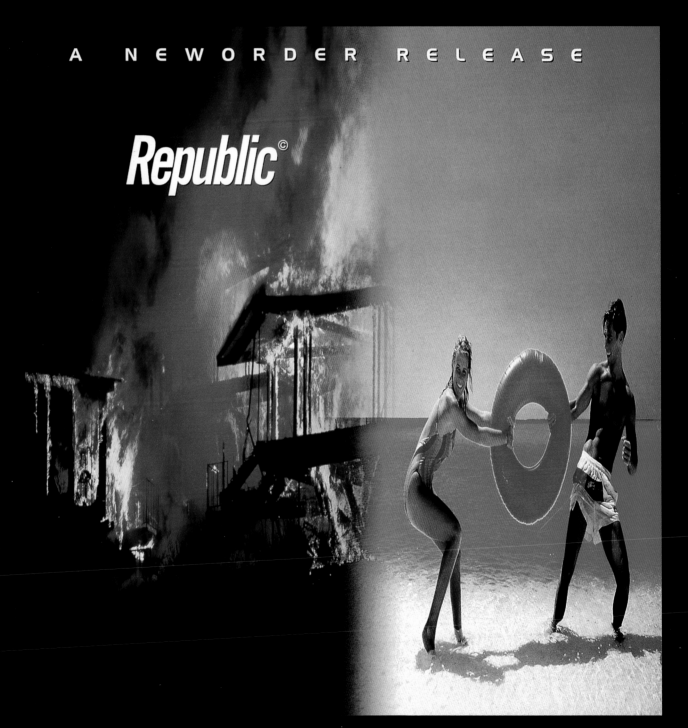

Het Loie Book
(The Oil Book)
Spreads from a book
about the uses and politics of oil
Designers: Gerard Hadders,
André van Dijk, Erik Prinsen
Design company: Hard Werken Design
Client: KVGO Printers Association
The Netherlands, 1991

Water stroomt altijd naar beneden, maar een glas is nog geen stuwmeer.

te van de aarde is heet

Heet water borrelt of spuit uit de grond maar is nog lang geen geiser in Spijkenisse.

in water schuilt kracht

De onderwereld brandt: het begint een nieuw leven als grondstof voor produkten en energiebehoeften

het zwarte goud gloeit

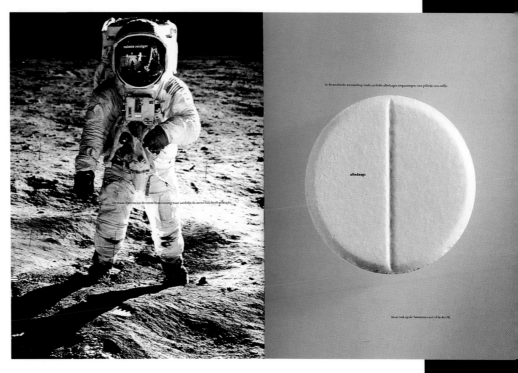

ruimte reiziger

De maan zegt nu toe de verste bestemming waar aardolie de mens ooit heeft gebracht.

In de medische wetenschap vindt aardolie alledaagse toepassingen: een pilletje, een zalfje.

alledaags

Maar ook op de 'intensive care' of in de OK.

Equilibrium Vessel:
The Phases of Water/The Faces of Man
Project for *Subjective Reasoning* magazine
Designers: Gerard Hadders, Allen Hori
Creative direction: Willem Kars
Design company: Hard Werken Design
Commissioning editors: William Drenttel, Paula Scher
Client: Champion International Corporation
USA, 1993

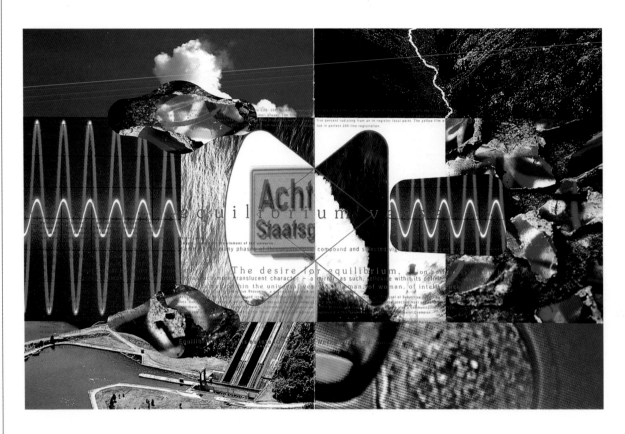

52° 5' N 5° 8' E 10.30 21 03 1941 N° 835

52°5' N 5°8' E 10.30 21031941 N° 835
Birthday book cover and spreads
Designer: Irma Boom
Photographer: Paul Fentener van Vlissingen
Client: Paul Fentener van Vlissingen
The Netherlands, 1991

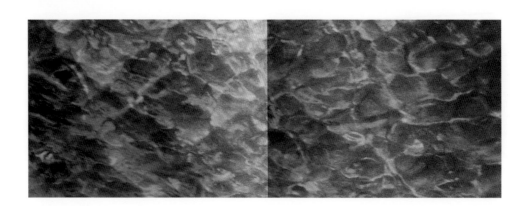

raw

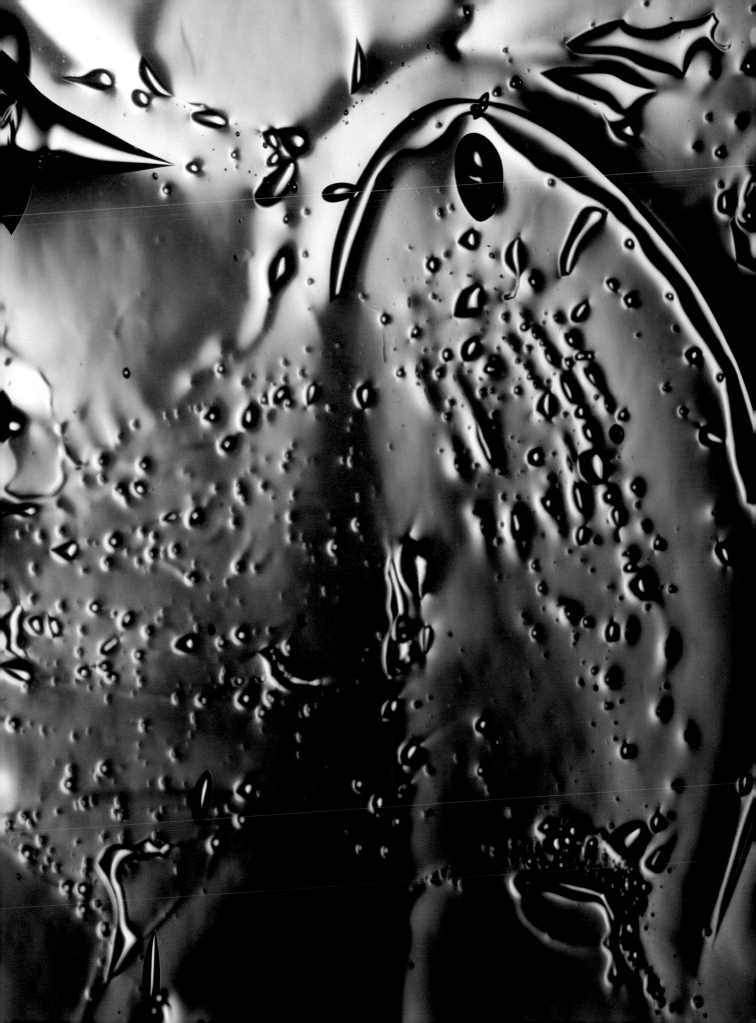

Concert posters
Designer: Michiel Uilen
Design company: Michiel Uilen Ontwerp
Client: de Salon, Groningen
The Netherlands, 1990-92

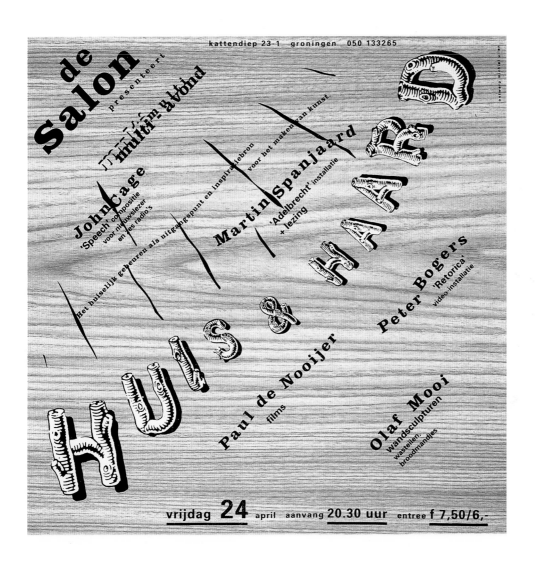

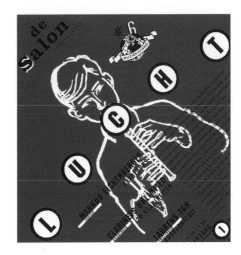

Brain-

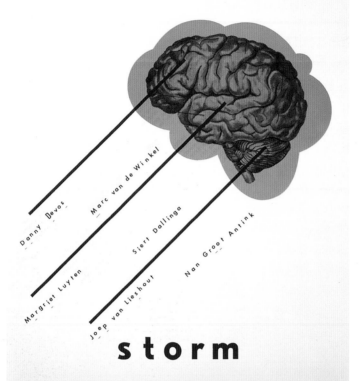

Danny Devos

Marc van de Winkel

Margriet Luyten

Siert Dallinga

Joep van Lieshout

Nan Groot Antink

storm

1 september - 23 september

opening: zaterdag 1 september 16.00 uur

openingstijden: do. t/m zo. 13.00 - 17.00 uur

artis

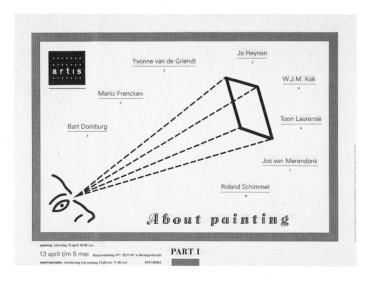

artis

Yvonne van de Griendt
3

Jo Heynen
4

W.J.M. Kok
5

Marliz Frencken
2

Toon Laurense
6

Bart Domburg
1

Jos van Merendonk
7

Roland Schimmel
8

About painting

opening: zaterdag 13 april 16.00 uur

13 april t/m 5 mei   Boschveldweg 471 5211 VK 's-Hertogenbosch

openingstijden: donderdag t/m zondag 13.00 t/m 17.00 uur   073 139052

PART I

Ellis Belier
Lidy Jacobs
Teuny Tukker
Stefan Axel Valdimarsson
Dieneke Vos
en leerlingen L.A.S. Hugo de Vries Rotterdam

met werken van

15 maart t/m 22 april
opening zondag 15 maart 15.00 - 18.00 uur
Wij heten U van harte welkom
de bloemenwinkel van Geer Pouls
Nieuwe Binnenweg 162
3015 BH Rotterdam
010 - 436 59 35
openingstijden:
dinsdag t/m vrijdag 11.00 - 18.00 uur
zaterdag 11.00 - 15.00 uur

Leo van Veldhuizen

Han Rameckers

Jer

Christie van der Ha

Ee

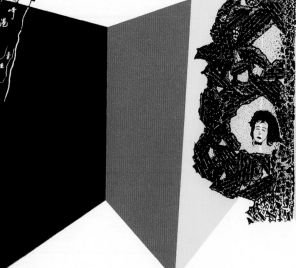

The Peace Museum

JOIN

PEACE EDUCATION through the arts and humanities

30 critically acclaimed exhibitions on issues related to war and peace

OTHER than DRAWINGS included in the **UNFORGETTABLE FIRE**, the FIRST U.S. EXHIBITION of ORIGINAL DRAWINGS by survivors of the Hiroshima and Nagasaki atomic bombings, at the **PEACE MUSEUM**.

peace

topics ranging from the life of Dr. Martin Luther King, Jr., to the role of popular music in efforts for social change, to the effect of war toys on children

the museum

430 West Erie Street
Chicago, IL 60610
312.440.1860

Advertisement
Designer: Joan Dobkin
Client: The Peace Museum
USA, 1991

Heads Up
Concert poster
Designers: Gerbrand van Melle
Design company: AAP Designers
Client: Tivoli, Utrecht
The Netherlands, 1991

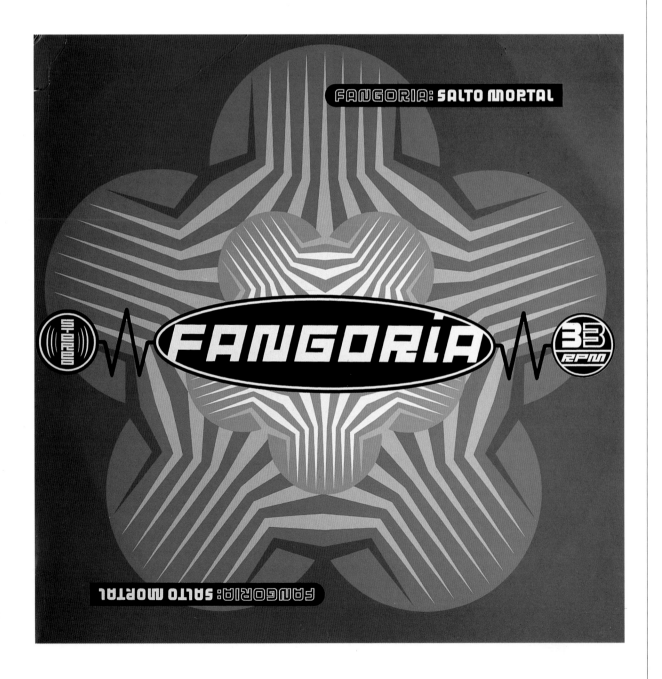

Salto Mortal
Album cover
Designers: Ian Anderson, David Smith
Design company: The Designers Republic
Client: EMI Hispavox
Great Britain, 1990

Gletcher Summer 1991
Brochure spreads
Designers: Armand Mevis, Linda van Deursen
Design company: Mevis & van Deursen
Client: Gletcher Fashion Designers
The Netherlands, 1990

Reason 2 Survive
Promotional poster
Designer: Simon Taylor
Design company: Tomato
Client: Diddley Daddy, Tokyo
Great Britain, 1992

Design?
Satirical poster campaign by Fresh UP,
a loose alliance of designers
Designer: Gerbrand van Melle
Design company: AAP Designers
Client: Horen, Zien & Vergaan, Rotterdam
The Netherlands, 1992

PhotoVideo
Exhibition poster
Designers: Richard Bonner-Morgan,
Kate Tregoning
Design company: Nice
Client: Impressions Gallery, York
Great Britain, 1991

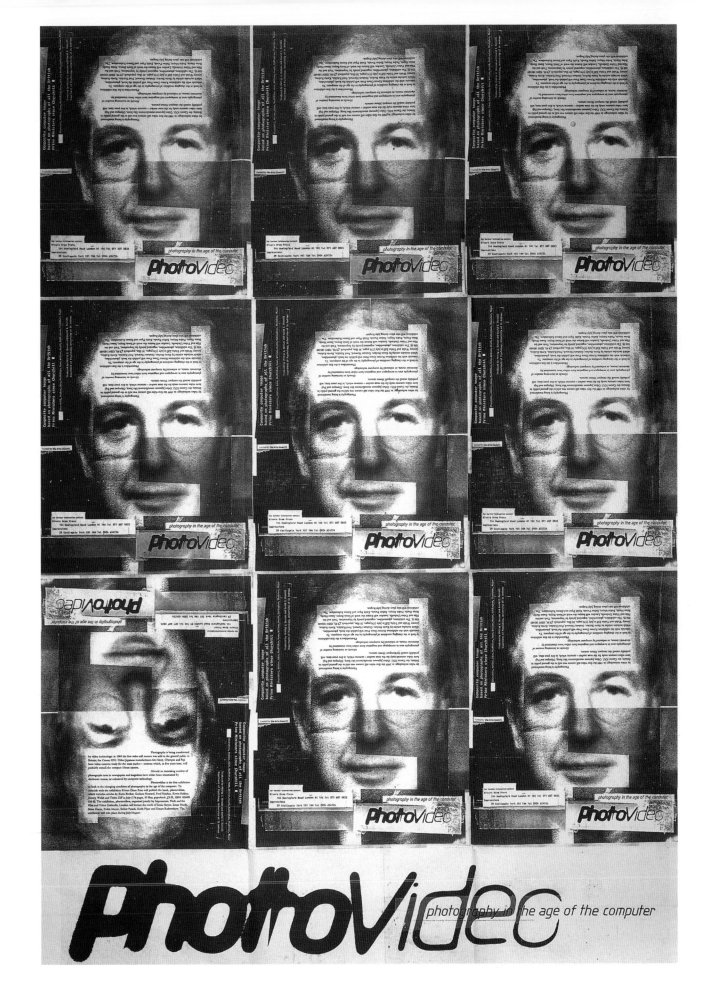

Tetsuo: The Iron Man
Film poster
Designer: A. Arefin
Client: Institute of Contemporary Arts,
London
Great Britain, 1991

Swoon
Film poster
Designers: Marlene McCarty, Donald Moffe
Design company: Bureau
Client: FineLine Features
USA, 1992

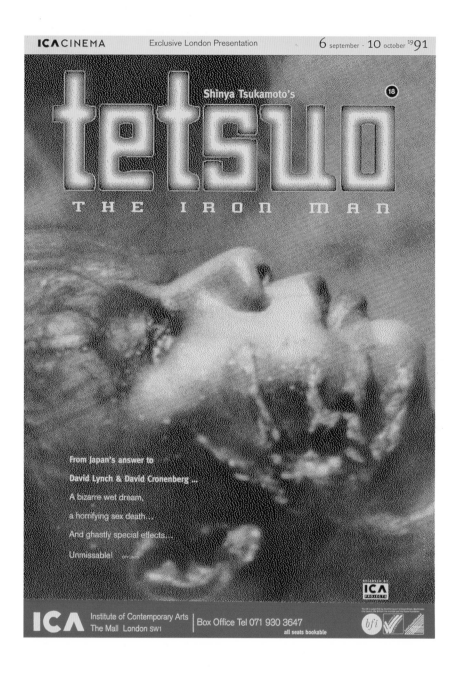

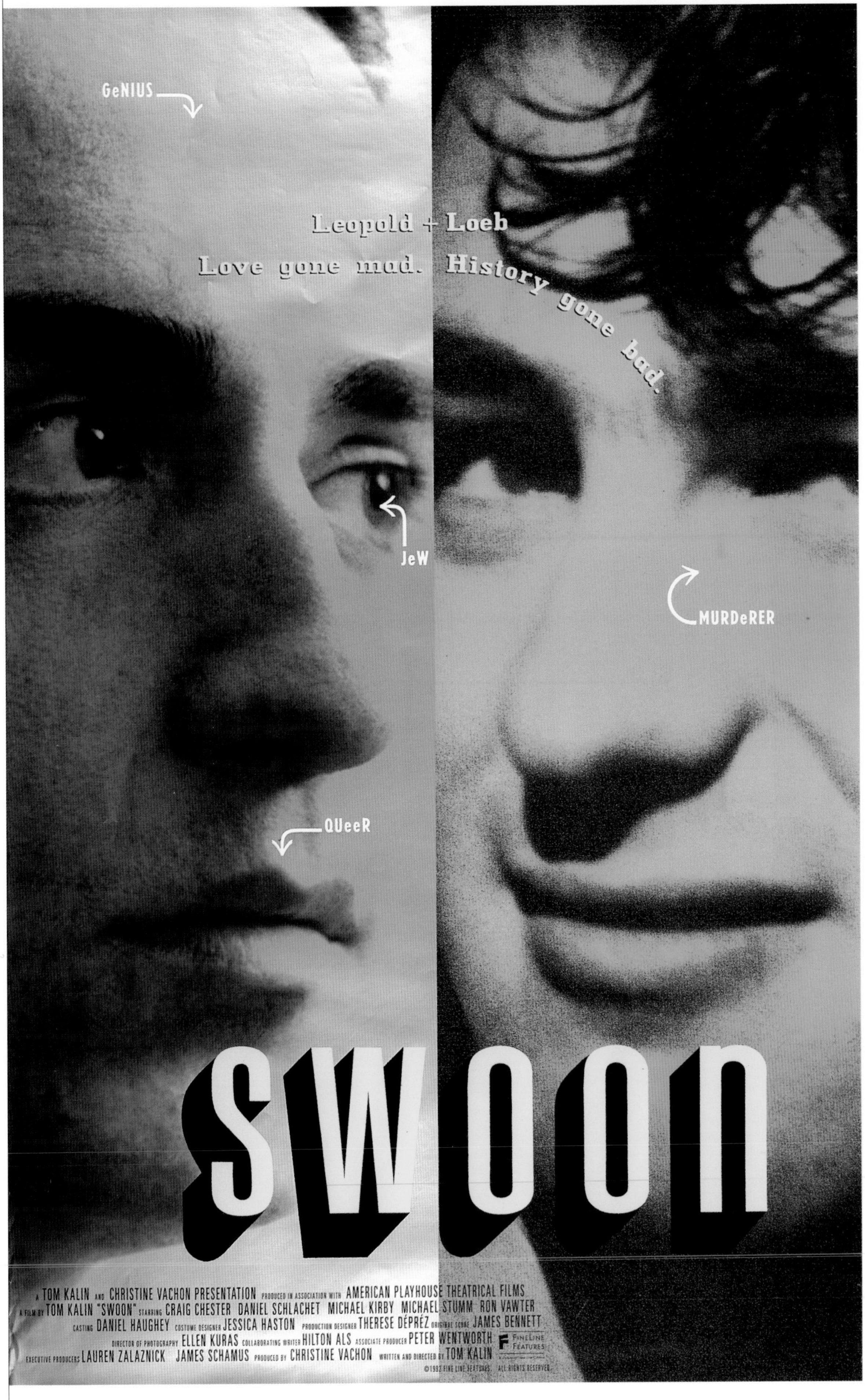
GeNIUS
Leopold + Loeb
Love gone mad. History gone bad.
JeW
MURDeRER
QUeeR
SWOON
A TOM KALIN AND CHRISTINE VACHON PRESENTATION PRODUCED IN ASSOCIATION WITH AMERICAN PLAYHOUSE THEATRICAL FILMS
A FILM BY TOM KALIN "SWOON" STARRING CRAIG CHESTER DANIEL SCHLACHET MICHAEL KIRBY MICHAEL STUMM RON VAWTER
CASTING DANIEL HAUGHEY COSTUME DESIGNER JESSICA HASTON PRODUCTION DESIGNER THERESE DÉPRÉZ ORIGINAL SCORE JAMES BENNETT
DIRECTOR OF PHOTOGRAPHY ELLEN KURAS COLLABORATING WRITER HILTON ALS ASSOCIATE PRODUCER PETER WENTWORTH
EXECUTIVE PRODUCERS LAUREN ZALAZNICK JAMES SCHAMUS PRODUCED BY CHRISTINE VACHON WRITTEN AND DIRECTED BY TOM KALIN
FINE LINE FEATURES
©1992 FINE LINE FEATURES. ALL RIGHTS RESERVED.

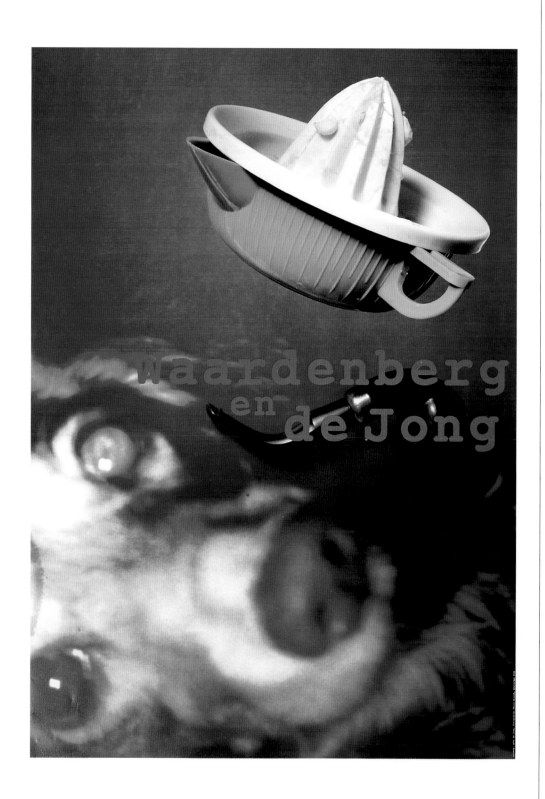

Theatre group poster
Design company: gebr de Jong
Photographers: gebr de Jong, Thijs Wolzak
Client: Waardenberg & de Jong
The Netherlands, 1991

Dutch Design/Industrial Design
Covers for a series of design books
Designers: Jacques Koeweiden, Paul Postma
Design company: Koeweiden Postma
Photographer: YANi
Client: BIS, Publishers
The Netherlands, 1992

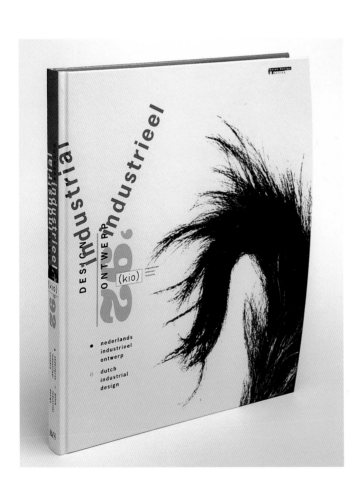

Theatre group poster
Design company: gebr de Jong
Photographers: gebr de Jong, Thijs Wolzak
Client: Waardenberg & de Jong
The Netherlands, 1991

Dutch Design/Industrial Design
Covers for a series of design books
Designers: Jacques Koeweiden, Paul Postma
Design company: Koeweiden Postma
Photographer: YANi
Client: BIS, Publishers
The Netherlands, 1992

Jool Hul
Theatre group poster
Design company: gebr de Jong
Photographers: gebr de Jong,
Dominique Pelletey
Client: Waardenberg & de Jong
The Netherlands, 1989

Star
Poster for an audiovisual display
Designer: Rana Salam
Self-published, Royal College of Art
Great Britain, 1992

Issue 4 Summer 1992

Fuel, issue 1, "Girl"
Magazine cover and spread
Designers: Peter Miles, Damon Murray,
Stephen Sorrell, Nick Oates
Design company: Fuel
Self-published, Royal College of Art
Great Britain, Spring 1991

Fuel, issue 4, "Cash"
Magazine cover and spread
Designers: Peter Miles, Damon Murray,
Stephen Sorrell
Design company: Fuel
Self-published, Royal College of Art
Great Britain, Summer 1992

MEAT

'The worst is not, so long as we can say 'This is the worst'...'
Mass-murderer Jeffrey Dahmer took such delight in his killing, such pride. He
used to keep people's heads in his fridge. Once, he showed them to an intended
victim. 'Aren't they beautiful' he said, as if he had sculpted and cast them himself.

There have been bigger killers, possibly even madder ones, than Dahmer, but
nothing beats that image for bone-chilling horror: human heads on the shelves of
a fridge, the same shelves on which the rest of America keeps its two pint cartons
of milk and Tropicana orange juice, its jars of pesto and Jell-o moulds.

Surely there could be nothing worse. There was nothing worse, until, that is, a
new horror story came out of Argentina this year. Directors and doctors at a
mental health institution near Buenos Aires were arrested on suspicion that
patients had been killed for spare parts. Evidence accumulated from exhumed
bodies suggested that eyes and other organs had been removed and blood
drained, and that these were then sold for cash. The body of a sixteen-year-old
boy was found at the bottom of a well with his eyes missing. He was supposed to
have 'escaped' from the institution, but he was totally paralysed and could not
even feed himself.

The workings of a lunatic's mind are terrible to think about. But sometimes the
workings of the free market manage to exceed them.

Richard Preston

MART

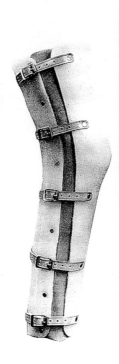

Fuel, issue 2, "Hype"
Magazine cover and spreads
Designers: Peter Miles, Damon Murray,
Stephen Sorrell, Nick Oates
Design company: Fuel
Self-published, Royal College of Art
Great Britain, Autumn 1991

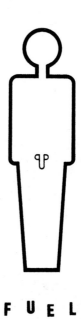

F U E L

"Yeah, lowered it, got the full kit on, Recaros, split rims, full spec, fully loaded - well sweet. Only got to sort the heads and we will be talking WELL rapid. The kitchen? Kitchen's done, sorted, so's the whole place now, top spec stuff. Miele Novotronic Hydromatic out the back and a Zanussi Jetsystem Turbodry, and the toaster's got a micro chip in it. Braun electronic sensor, but who gives a shit about toast eh, do me a favour! Electrolux? Stroll on! The only one they DO is the 1200 watt Superboost and that's for some sort of dwarf. What you want is a Hoover Turbomaster - wicked black finish, drop a body kit on it you could practically DRIVE it. Debenhams credit all the way, sweet stuff. Went up there last week, she got herself a Clairol Turbo but I really rated the Braun - the

SPEC

Silencio 1600 - oof! The dog's COCK. It's what Gary Lineker uses, a mate of mine told me. Switch that and the Clairol on together it's like you're in some serious sort of wind tunnel. Picked a portable system too - ALMOST got the Philips with the Turbo Bass Generator, but it had to be that JVC, you know, the PC-X300 - no, NOT the 300 Bazza you PLONKER - Hyper-Bass, Live Effex, choice or WHAT. Next up it's got to be one of their CDs, check the spec on this: 'XL-E44, PEM DD Converter - Pulse Edge Modulation Differential Linearity Errorless D/A'. Sweet as a NUT. Oof! Who's guffed then? I reckon when I pump it's turbocharged - a real twenty-four valve, gold-plated special - I was touching cloth for a minute there. So anyway, I s'pose a shag's out of the question?"

Richard Preston
Assistant Editor, Harpers and Queen

WARNING
THIS PLANCE
MUST BE EARTHED

The Cornflake Shop

37 Windmill Street London W1P 1HH
071 631 0472 Fax 071 436 7165

Earth Warning
Promotional poster
Designer: Paul Elliman
Client: The Cornflake Shop
Great Britain, 1992

Richard II
Theatre poster
Designer: Paul Elliman
Photographer: Donald Cooper
Client: Royal Shakespeare Company
Great Britain, 1991

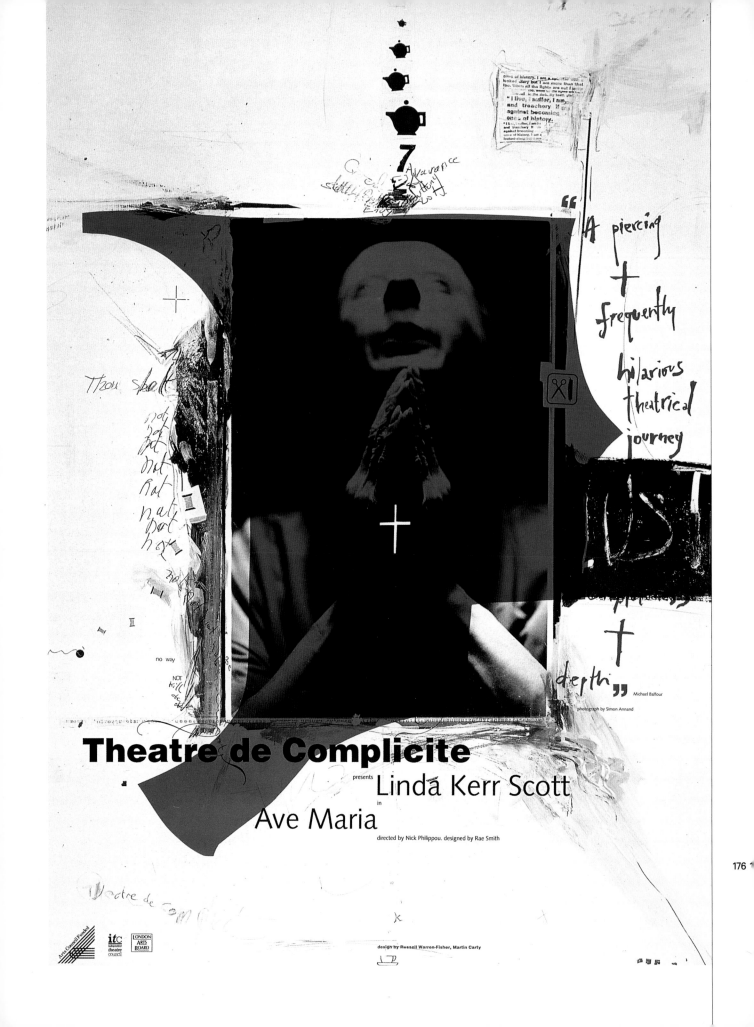

"A piercing † frequently hilarious theatrical journey

depth"

Michael Balfour

photograph by Simon Annand

Theatre de Complicite

presents Linda Kerr Scott

in

Ave Maria

directed by Nick Philippou. designed by Rae Smith

design by Russell Warren-Fisher, Martin Carty

Ave Maria
Theatre poster
Designers: Russell Warren-Fisher, Martin Carty
Photographers: Simon Annand,
Gareth McCarthy
Illustrator: Martin Carty
Client: Theatre de Complicite
Great Britain, 1992

Ray Charles: My World
CD cover
Designer: P. Scott Makela
Design company: P. Scott Makela Words +
Pictures for Business + Culture
Client: Warner Brothers Records
USA, 1992

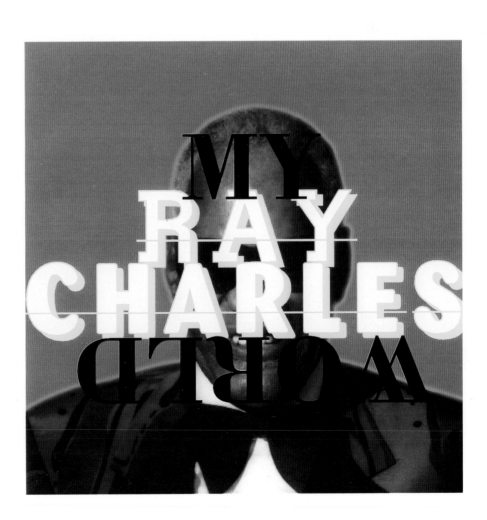

music +style
(the bible of)

rAY
GUn

PREMIERE ISSUE

henry rollins
sonic youth
house of love
inspiral carpets
john wesley
harding
the lemonheads
luna
opus 111
the prodigy
mary's danish
mission k
too much joy
david j
matt mahurin

one november 1992
$3.50 u.s. $3.95 canada

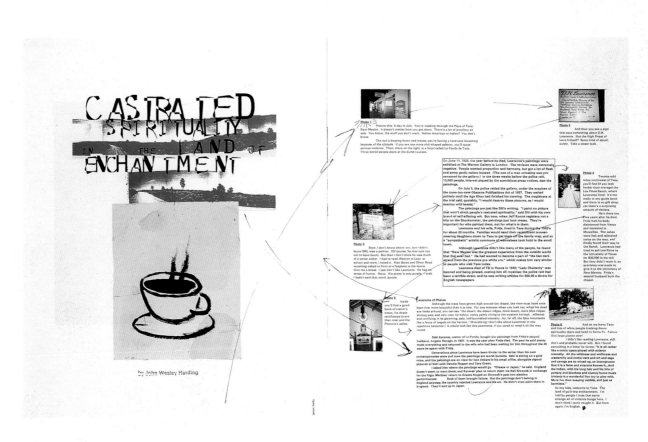

Ray Gun, issue 3
Magazine spread
Designer: David Carson
Photographer: Anthony Artiago
Client: Ray Gun Publishing
USA, 1992

Ray Gun, issue 4
Magazine spread
Designer: David Carson
Illustrator: Amy Guip
Client: Ray Gun Publishing
USA, 1993

Ray Gun, issue 2
Magazine spread
Designer: David Carson
Client: Ray Gun Publishing
USA, 1992

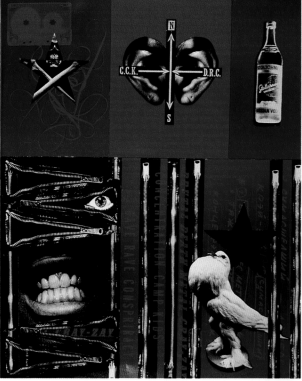

Light
Reading
THE MAN ON THE

MOON

by
Peter
Care

101.01.18

01.00.20.14

Last fall R.E.M. began filming *Man On The Moon*, one of the most cinematically complicated videos it or any other band has attempted. What follows is an inside look at how a music video is made, from the director's own notes.

e side of my head

rts

om thinking in the rain

Jack Kerouac Remix as sampled and scratched by Elliott Peter Earls

My Head Hurts
Poster
Designer/photographer: Elliott Peter Earls
Self-published, Cranbrook Academy of Art
USA, 1992

Exhibition poster
Designer: Anne Burdick
Photographer: Julie Becker
Client: Julie Becker
USA, 1991

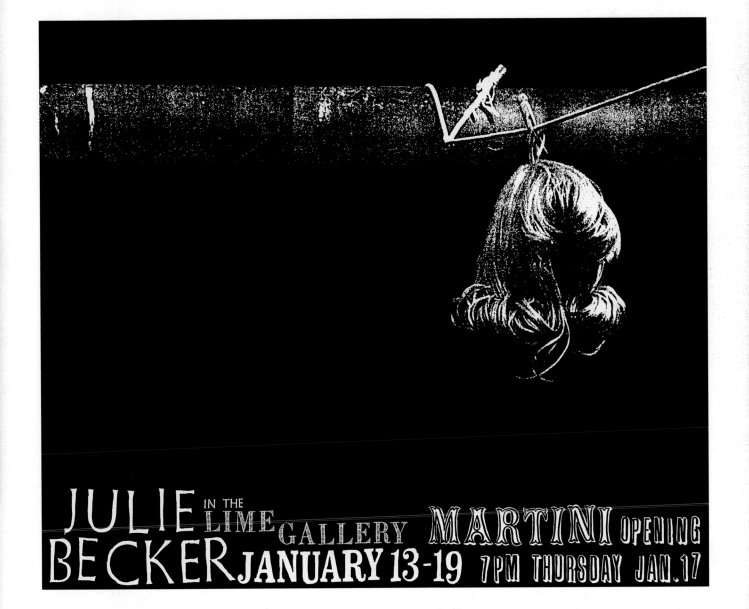

Ramona 55
Record sleeve
Designer: Graham Wood
Design company: Tomato
Client: Electric Wonderland Records
Great Britain, 1992

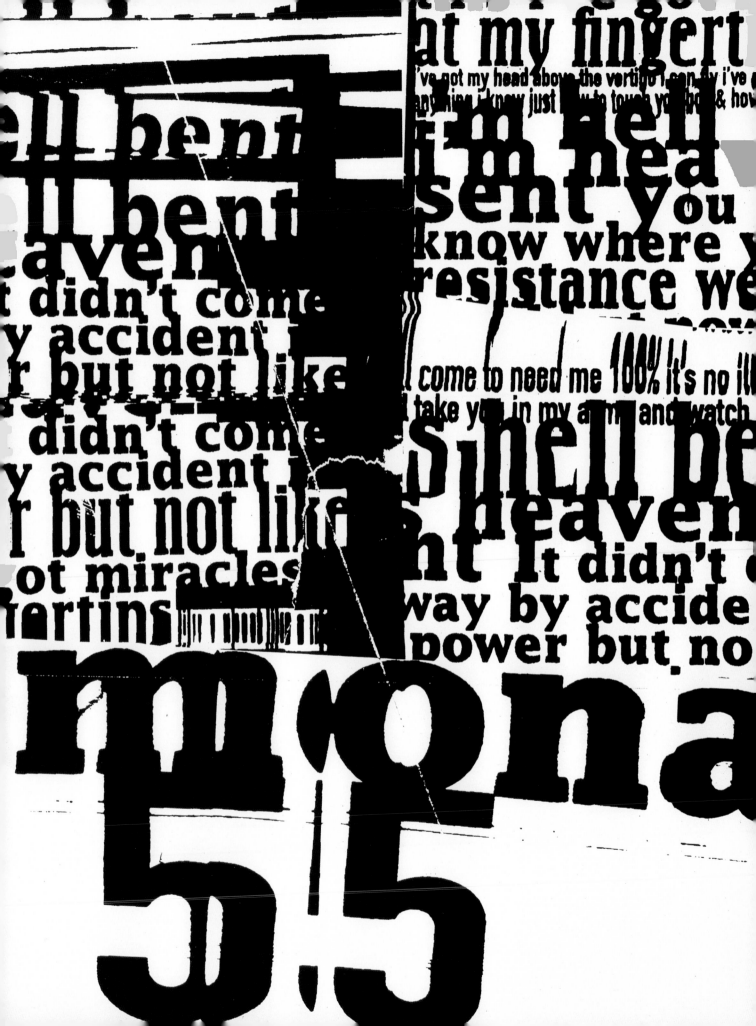

My name is Dita.
I'll be your mistress tonight.
I'll be your loved one, darling.
Turn out the light.
I'll be your sorceress,
your heart's magician.
I'm not a witch.
I'm a love technician.
I'll be your guiding light
in your darkest hour.
I'm gonna change your life.
I'm like a poison flower.
Give it up.
Do as I say.
Give it up and let me have my way.
I'll give you love.
I'll hit you like a truck.
I'll give you love......

Sex by Madonna
Book spreads
Designer: Fabien Baron
Design company: Baron & Baron
Photographer: Steven Meisel
Client: Warner Books
USA, 1992

Sex by Madonna
Book spreads
Designer: Fabien Baron
Design company: Baron & Baron
Photographer: Steven Meisel
Client: Warner Books
USA, 1992

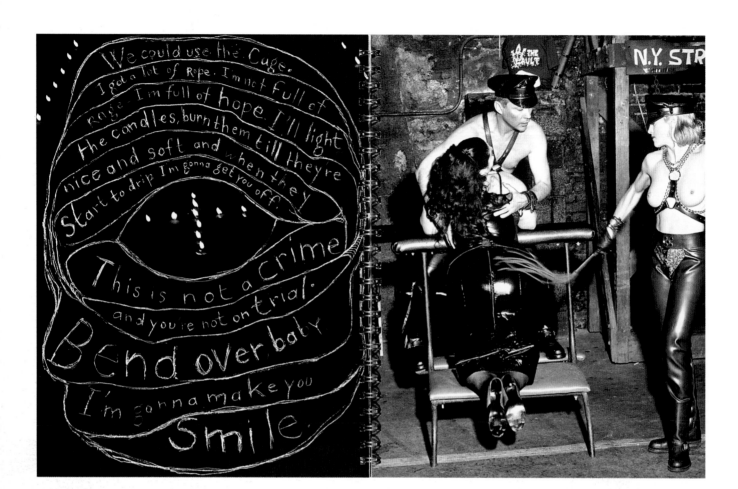

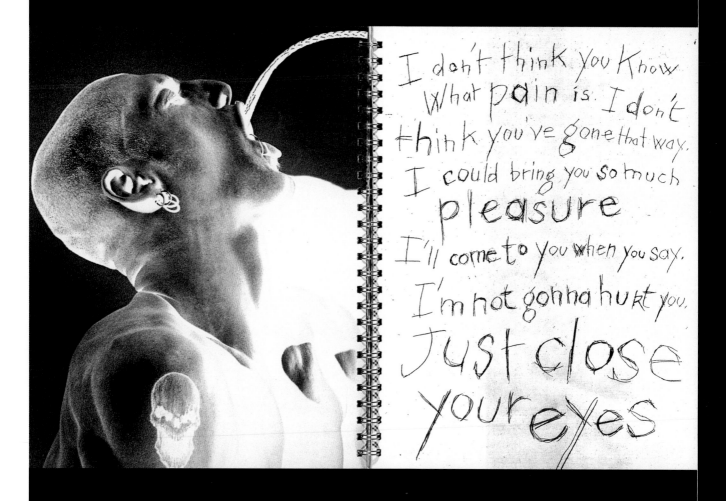

Is FASHION dead?

Pam Hogg, Anthony Price, Joe Casely Hayford, Body Map, John Galliano, ALLY CAPELLINo, Nicola Georgiou, No Moths in our Wardrobe

A series of talks in which top British Designers discuss the relevance and significance of fashion in the late '80s ● Tickets £2.60 (plus ICA Daypass £1.00) ● Institute of Contemporary Arts, The Mall, London SW1Y 5AH Box Office 01-930 3647.

ICA

present times

From chaos and danger. . . opportunity.

Helen Storey Autumn/Winter 1991 Collection

Is Fashion Dead?
Leaflet
Designers: Moira Bogue, Tim Hopgood
Design company: Bogue & Hopgood
Client: Institute of Contemporary Arts, London
Great Britain, 1989

Present Times
Fashion show programme
Designer: Moira Bogue
Design company: Bogue & Hopgood
Client: Helen Storey
Great Britain, 1991

Darling
Book jacket
Designer/photographer: Chip Kidd
Client: Alfred A. Knopf
USA, 1992

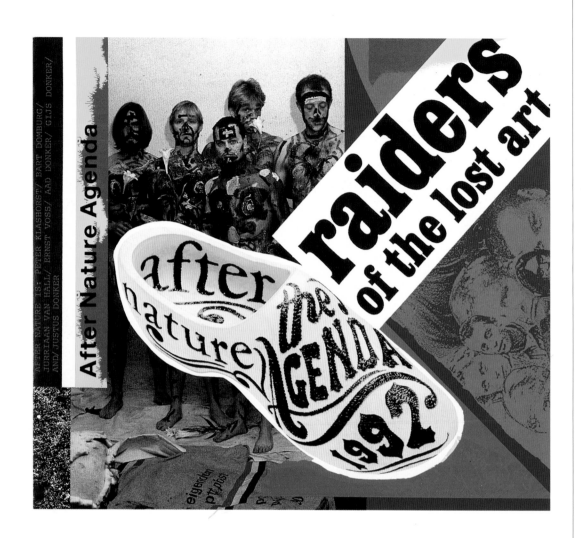

AFTER NATURE IS: PETER KLASHORST/ BART DOMBURG/ JURRIAAN VAN HALL/ ERNST VOSS/ AAD DONKER/ GIJS DONKER/ AND/ JUSTUS DONKER

After Nature Agenda

Raiders of the Lost Art
1992 diary cover
Designers: Armand Mevis, Linda van Deursen
Design company: Mevis & van Deursen
Client: After Nature
The Netherlands, 1991

NowTime, issue 2
Magazine cover
Designers: Somi Kim, Lisa Nugent, Whitney
Lowe, Susan Parr, Lorraine Wild, Caryn Aono
Design company: ReVerb/Los Angeles
Client: *NowTime*/A.R.T. Press
USA, 1992

"Any place I hang
my hat is home
sweet home to
me."

Information Hotline
1-800-7223765

USC

DEANS' HALL   HONORS HOUSING TWO

At USC, students come from all different places.
And they study all kinds of subjects. But when they are
in Deans' Hall they all call it home.

BUSINESS REPLY MAIL
FIRST-CLASS MAIL   PERMIT NO. 95228   LOS ANGELES, CA
POSTAGE WILL BE PAID BY ADDRESSEE

NO POSTAGE
NECESSARY
IF MAILED
IN THE
UNITED STATES

ATTN DEAN'S HALL
UNIVERSITY OF SOUTHERN CALIFORNIA
P.O. BOX 77902
LOS ANGELES, CA 90099-3334

CalArts Dance
Poster
Designer: Caryn Aono
Design company: CalArts Public Affairs Office
Photographer: Steven A. Gunther
Client: CalArts
USA, 1991

T-Zone
Architectural catalogue cover
Designers: Andy Altmann, David Ellis,
Christopher Priest
Design company: Why Not Associates
Client: Design Analysis International
Great Britain, 1991

faculty:

CristyneLawson, Dean
  LarryAttaway, Associate Dean
 RebeccaBobele, Assistant Dean
LaurenceBlake
  ClareDuncan
 JacquesHeim
  HirokoHojo
   DavidKroth
  RobertOchs
MichaelRoberts
   KurtWeinheimer
  TinaYuan

CalArts

dance

audition dates:

Phoenix Jan 21
San Francisco Feb 1
Portland Feb 3
Houston Feb 7
Atlanta Feb 8
Minneapolis Feb 12
Baltimore Feb 14
Chicago Feb 15
New York City Feb 17
Washington DC Feb 20
Los Angeles Jan 18 at CalArts
Los Angeles Feb 22 at CalArts
Los Angeles Mar 7 at CalArts

Admission to CalArts is based on talent.

Applicants to the performing arts programs must audition.

California Institute of the Arts offers Bachelor of Fine Arts and Master of Fine Arts degrees, as well as certificate and advanced certificate programs, in its schools of Art, Dance, Film/Video, Music, and Theatre. The Institute's Division of Critical Studies provides the academic courses required of students in the BFA degree program.

Contact:
Office of Admissions
CalArts
24700 McBean Parkway
Valencia, CA 91355

Anyone interested in applying for any kind of financial assistance should contact the Office of Financial Aid well before the March 1, deadline each year.

toll free:
1-800-292-ARTS
(in CA)
1-800-545-ARTS
(other states)

Financial Aid
toll free:
1-800-443-0480

California Institute of the Arts is accredited by the Accrediting Commission for Senior Colleges and Universities of the Western Association of Schools and Colleges. The Institute's School of Dance is an accredited institutional member of the National Association of Schools of Dance.

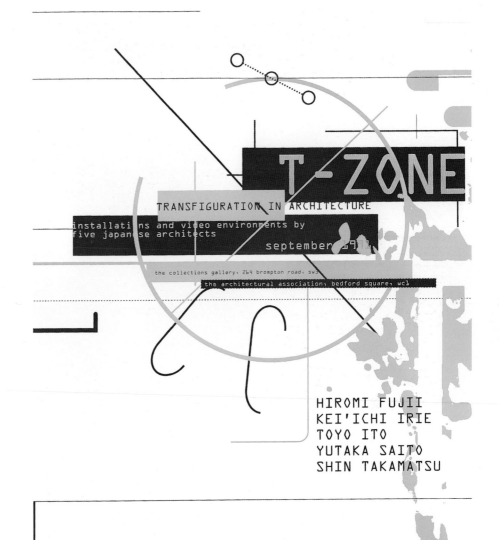

T-ZONE

TRANSFIGURATION IN ARCHITECTURE

installations and video environments by
five japanese architects

september 1991

the collections gallery, 264 brompton road, sw3

the architectural association, bedford square, wc1

HIROMI FUJII
KEI'ICHI IRIE
TOYO ITO
YUTAKA SAITO
SHIN TAKAMATSU

CalArts'

17th WoRld mUSic feStiVal '91

In MemOry Of TArAnAth RAO

NORtH INDiAn MuSiC StuDents & AluMni __fri Apr26__ 3pm MAiN Gallery
NOrtH INDIAn MusIc with TaLa VadYa __8pm MoDuIar THeatre__

StudEnt JAvAnese GaMeIAn __sat Apr27__ 5pm MaiN gallery
AFRICAn MusIc & DaNCe __8pm mODuIar theatRe__

ClAssical JaPANese MUsiC __Sun Apr28__ 4pm ThEaTRe II
LATiN-AMeRICAn MuSiC __8pm moDuIaR thEatre__

ClaSsical JApANesE DaNCE __fri May3__ 5pm tHEAtRe II
SOUtH INdIAn MusIc & DaNCe __8pm modUIar ThEatre__

StUdeNt AFRiCAn MuSIC & DaNCe __5pm mAIn gallery__
BAlIneSe MuSIC & dAnce with KecaK (monkey chant) __sat May4__ 8pm moDuIar theaTRE
New PACIfiC __11pm MAiN GalleRy__

MIdDLE-EAsTern musiC & danCe __sun May5__ 4pm MaiN GalerY
JaVAnese MuSIC & dance __8pm modUIar theatrE__

8 pm P E R F O R Mances: $ 6 general. $ 3 students/seniors. OTHeR PERFormances: F R E E.
6 pm D I Nners: $ 6 /person.
I N F O R Mation: (818) 3 6 2 - 2 3 1 5 or (805) 2 5 3 - 7 8 0 0.
C A L iFORnia Institute of the A R T S 24700 MCBean PARKway, ValenCIA, C A Lifornia

CalArts' 17th World
Music Festival '91
Poster
Designer: Caryn Aono
Design company: CalArts Public Affairs Office
Client: CalArts
USA, 1991

LAX: The Los Angeles Exhibition 1992
Catalogue cover and map insert
Designers: Somi Kim, Whitney Lowe,
Lisa Nugent
Design company: ReVerb/Los Angeles
Photographer: Andrew Bush
Map illustrator: Edward Fella
Client: Municipal Art Gallery, Los Angeles
USA, 1992

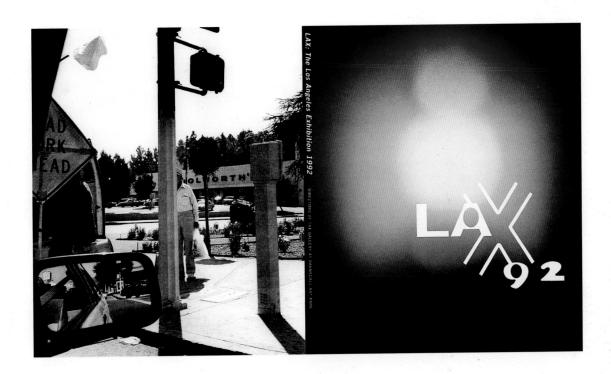

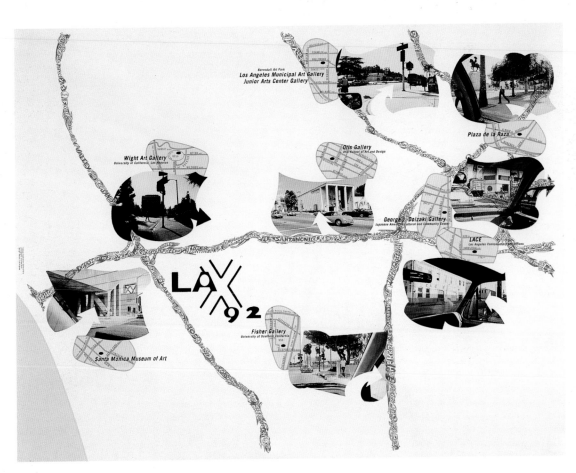

mark STRAND '91

4 -6pm
Wednesday,
NOv. 6

voice lying next to me.

and I hear my own

Poetry Today's erie/s
of Critical Studies

Langley HALL
CALIFORNIA INSTITUTE OF THE ARTS

POET LAUREATE *of the* United States

My body lies down

Excerpt from Darker. "Seven Poems." 4

Event posters
Designer: Gail Swanlund
Design company: CalArts Public Affairs Office
Client: CalArts
USA, 1991, 1992

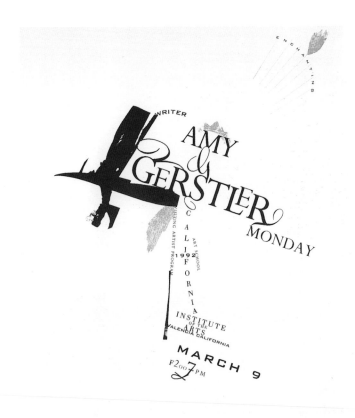

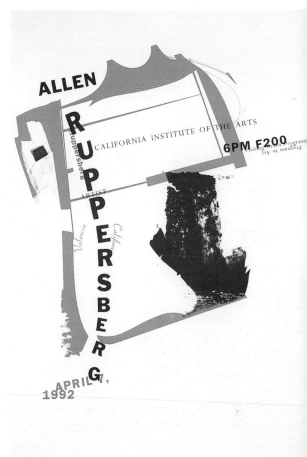

The ART School
(is)
FINALLY GIVING A
Party
(to)
WELCOME
Tom Lawson

on Sunday, DECEMBER 6 * Snow date: the following Sunday, dec. 13TH 1992

Please Come and bring A guest DRESS WARMLY!
between 2 AND 3 p.m. (early Supper-5 p.m.)
live Music

at Nancy MITCHNICK's Studio near GORMAN Compound. LARGE surrounded BY A CYCLONE fence Surrounded by Mountains
on highway 138, ½ MILE PAST N2 ROAD
(4 MI. OFF I-5)

CALARTS
SCHOOL OF
ART
PROGRAM
IN GRAPHIC DESIGN
DESIGNED
&ILLUSTRATED
FELLA RT
24700 MC BEAN
PKWY VALENCIA
CA 91355

NO PROFIT ORG
U.S. POSTAGE
PAID
VALENCIA, CA
PERMIT#18

TO

index

what price dory?

what price dory?

by Chon Day

with text by Alfred F. Loomis

GILBERT PRESS, INC.

Distributed by Julian Messner, Inc.

Published by Gilbert Press, Inc.
A Subsidiary of Julian Messner, Inc.
8 West 40th St., New York 18

Published Simultaneously in Canada
by The Copp Clark Company, Ltd.

© Copyright 1955 by Chon Day

Library of Congress Catalog Card No. 55-9851

Printed in the United States of America

Foreward by Chon Day

Possibly the first boating was experienced by a caveman who rode a log down-stream in search of a mate or to escape from one. No doubt, he wondered then how nice it might be if he could ride it upstream without an oar. Our friend never gave seamanship nor yachtsmen's clothing much thought in those days. He merely wanted maritime transportation, and got it.

In this book, you will see people, yourself maybe, in various aqueous activities, none of which will help you in the least to become a navigator. The purpose of this published work is quite elusive, but it does indicate, sort of, a personal association of boats and gags. Naturally, no responsibility is assumed, and if names and situations fit you—you're stuck with them, and I'll move to Block Island.

If you have ever rented a canoe in a park; sailed in a tunnel of love; floated soap in your bath; stirred ice in a drink; or if you like boats, or breathe—then you have a good reason to own this book.

I am exceedingly grateful to the United States Navy, Coast Guard and U. S. Power Squadrons for allowing me to use boats on the following pages.

Even More Foreward

by Alfred F. Loomis

It is becoming less and less possible (and more and more impossible if I may be permitted to look at both sides of the subject) to avoid yachts and yachtsmen. They are everywhere. Putting it even less succinctly, there is nowhere where they are not. If in order to avoid them you take a steamer to somewhere they will flag you down in mid-ocean. Conversely, if you seek out a secluded rill in the heart of a forest primeval you will see its mirror-like surface shattered by an enthusiastic outboard motorist. When Uncle Sam builds a dam for electrical purposes the water has barely time to electrify before there is a fleet of sail boats racing in it.

Other examples could be cited, but enough has been said to indicate that there is no escape. If you don't want to feel socially insecure you must learn to yacht. You must know the language which sets yachtsmen apart from reasonable people. You must know something of their methods and about the instruments they use to indulge their folly. In short, you must read this book as well as look at the pictures.

Your First Boat

YOUR FIRST BOAT

There are only three types of boats. Or two if you don't like rowboats. Of course, there are big and little boats as well as expensive and I was going to say inexpensive ones, but we'll skip that. While doing so I'll conclude that you have decided against a motor boat and have bought a cozy sail boat which is 72 feet in length from stem to stern or vice versa according to how you look at her. It is necessary to call a boat a she and this one would have cost you only $250,000 if you had bought her before prices went up.

Anybody who can afford all that money for a boat is an intuitive yachtsman and you have now sailed her to a little harbor far, far from city traffic and suburban ranch-type split-level TV sets. You have also anchored her, having first remembered to attach a line to the anchor—which some don't.

It is dusk. Twenty-seven other recluses have gotten away from it all in the same harbor, together with their wives, children, lady and gentleman friends, twenty-eight radios and one marmoset, and the twilight is filled with the darting silver pencils of brilliant searchlights. It is an idyllic scene if ever I described one.

The air is filled with joyous, raucous laughter, harmony, cacophony, commercials, an unguarded scream and the heavenly resonance of cocktail shakers.

The water is filled with inadvertent swimmers, grapefruit rinds, one marmoset and oil pumped from bilges.

The barometer falls, the wind rises until it drowns out the radios and you thank your lucky stars you have put yourself where there are no falling trees to endanger you.

The hurricane strikes and now you have no boat.

"Goodness, no. We're looking for a good, used
twelve foot skiff"

"Customer off the port bow, sir."

"Why, I used the CO₂ to cool the beer!"

"About five steps backward should do it."

"I built it myself."

"We've got ten minutes to kill."

"Does it have power brakes?"

The man who left his oars at the bottom of the boat

"I'm taking command here."

Art of anchoring

Low tide

Outboard Motor Cruisers

OUTBOARD MOTOR CRUISERS

The more fool you for not buying a complete little 23½-foot motor cruiser with twin outboard engines, high cruising speed, low maintenance cost and sleeping accommodations for six for $1576.00. Let us look closely at this intriguing situation.

The invention of the popular portable motor was the answer to the lazy boatman's prayer. He had gotten tired of rowing a row boat and so he changed pace and got tired trying to start the motor. Sometimes when the wind shifted in the middle of the day he blew back by evening to where he had started from in the morning. (Thus was the sail boat also invented.) Those early outboard motorists have now come ashore where they apply their vast experience to the starting of power lawn-mowers. When the grass needs cutting they hire a man.

In the meantime the best outboard motors have improved in all particulars except portability. They are bigger, quieter and more reliable, and as they even have electric starters I have no further objection to them. A few outboards having been lost overboard, there is now a trend toward bringing them inboard and mounting them in wells. With gear shifts, remote control, push button starting, separate fuel tanks and underwater exhausts they resemble inboard motors in everything except appearance. When that detail has been licked the outboards can be installed below decks where the inboards always were.

This will be, however, at the sacrifice of room now devoted to living—or at least existing—accommodations. How could you find room for six full length bunks in a 23½-footer if the engines occupied the better part of the main cabin? Where would you put the ice box and storage battery, to say nothing of the full length hanging lockers? How could six people keep out of one another's way unless they were in bed or in the privacy of their own homes where they'd be much better off? How could you have a toilet and a galley sink unless one drained into the other—I mean, unless the other drained into one? Who would navigate a lovely, commodious boat like this if he couldn't spread his charts on the stove at meal times?

Let it be understood once and for all that I'm asking and not answering these interesting questions.

Custom-Built Jobs

CUSTOM-BUILT JOBS

If, instead of buying a stock boat, you want a custom-built job it is important to secure the services of a naval architect. No fooling, you can't just step over to your drawing board and design a yacht that will be comfortable, seaworthy, and inexpensive without having had some experience along that line. The naval architect has had that experience.

So you go to him and say, "Look, John" [or Olin, Phil, Jack, Carl, Aage or Bill as the case may be. I'm not supposed to know the naval architects that you call by their first names]. You say, "Look, Tore, I want you to design me a boat. I'm a great one for cruising and don't give a hang about racing. I've been reading in the yachting magazine that the coming thing is the obsolete gaff-rigged schooner, and that's what I want. She's gotter be 35 feet in length and I want a lotter beam and draft. Tons of living accommodations for my growing family and the galley aft so my wife can stand there and talk to me while I'm steering. Sturdy Diesel engine with three-bladed prop. I'll pay $8,999.00."

The N.A. looks you straight in the eye and says, "I know exactly what you have in mind because I've designed a lot of successful boats to those specifications. But this will have those little marks of distinction which will make her a member of your family. Leave it to me."

Pretty soon you have a chance to look at the lines, accommodation plan, sail plan, table of offsets, etc., and I don't need to tell you that you will be delighted with everything about the boat. You may, however, be a little surprised at the result, for in place of your stipulations this is what you've got: A lean, jib-headed yawl 40 feet over all of keel-centerboard type drawing very little water. She has bunks for three in port or for six when racing, and instead of a big Diesel there is a little high-speed gasoline motor with reduction gear turning a two-bladed feathering wheel. The motor is so conveniently located that to get at it all you have to do is remove the revolving galley. To do that you lift off the chart table, which you can very easily do if the navigator isn't sleeping on his mattress on top of it. Getting a can of beer is still easier. The cost of the entire boat will be about $40,000, but you should have known that in that one teeny weeny respect you wouldn't get your heart's desire.

As I wouldn't want you to think I'm being cynical in this important matter of fitting the right boat to the right person I'll tell you this: The boat will be so beautiful that at the launching the designer will think she was designed by one of his competitors. And she'll go like smoke and win races wherever she is sailed.

But you don't like racing and wanted a roomy, comfortable family cruiser? Don't be ridiculous. A boat like the one you had in mind will have absolutely no resale value.

"I can make a very attractive offer if you care to buy two."

Yakkety-Yak

YAKKETY-YAK

When a group of yachtsmen start talking things over pretty soon one of them will wiggle a thumb and two fingers to imitate the opening and shutting of a mouth and will say "Yakkety-yak." This indicates that they have gotten around to Topic A with relation to boats and that while the little dears have their uses they talk too much.

Within the memory of the older generation of yachtsmen women were only allowed aboard yachts as ornaments or pets. Recently, however, a few rugged pioneers who had been threatened with writs of habeas corpus if they didn't stay home, now and then got into the way of taking their wives off on cruises. The idea spread like wildfire and now in a popular anchorage you will rarely see a cruising boat that is not graced and beautified by the fair sex. (Yakkety-yak.)

And no wonder. Whose ear has been trained to pick up unusual noises in the dead of night? Mother's. ("All right, dear, and since you're up why don't you give the anchor cable more scope and close the hatch to keep out the rain?")

We don't have to ask who lights the fire, boils coffee and eggs, folds the blankets, sweeps up and rows ashore to purchase the meat and groceries that were forgotten in the flurry of starting the cruise.

Very well, then, who struggles with the windlass, gets the anchor aboard and swabs down the deck? Mom. ("It isn't so much that I have to favor my back, darling, but that this is a crowded harbor and I wouldn't want you to run the risk of colliding with another boat. Besides, you said you needed the exercise to keep your tummy flat.")

Who studies the charts, Coast Pilot and Light List and lays out the courses for the day's run? The little woman. ("You see, sweetheart, there's always the chance of my falling overboard and you know how helpless you would feel if you hadn't mastered the art of piloting.")

Who takes the wheel while the other goes below for a pipe? Mother, who thereupon steers until it's time for lunch and dinner.

But after the boat is snugged down for the night who asks the gang aboard for drink and song? (And, hours later, says, "Now listen, darling, the least you can do is be hospitable when friends come aboard. Maybe I shouldn't have suggested scrambled eggs at midnight—but how was I to know they'd stick around till three a.m.? As long as I bear all the responsibility and do nine-tenths of the work you can make an effort to stay awake and be good natured.")

All the quoted words, in case you hadn't guessed it, were Father's. Yakkety-yak.

"You're in luck. I'm a millionaire."

". . . and this is the head."

"Would you have any idea where I might locate someone who
is stowing away?"

"How about cooking the mess?"

"You needn't think I'm going to cook that."

1

2

3

4

5

6

"Wife, I believe."

"I had hoped you were a cod."

Nautical Terms

Dead reckoning – A method of navigating

Port-red sherry

"Ahoy, there!"

Nautical Terms   Abeam – On the side of the vessel

"Oh, .er . . . Gob!"

"S.O.S.! S.O.S.!"

Signaling

Distress

Rules of the Road

"I take possession of this land in the name of
Horace P. Fritchie . . . me."

"I'm taking down that number."

"Uh, uh, uh . . ."

"I believe I had the right of way, old man."

"Ahoy! Could you spare some Vermouth?"

Getting Under Way

GETTING UNDER WAY

The way boat-handling instructions are usually written, the novice is pictured as finding himself starting off under the simplest conditions imaginable. For instance, in the getting-under-way situation his boat lies at the end of a pier which is unobstructed by boats or swimmers. Slack tide, no wind. A bill-collector comes along and all the novice has to do is start the motor, cast off mooring lines and he's off.

As you can't learn anything that way, let us begin with a more typical situation. There are no swimmers, for the reason that the weather is very cold for that time of year. It is cold because there is a strong wind blowing. The wind blows along the face of a T-shaped wharf, making it comparatively simple for the several boats that are moored there to get under way. But our boat, a twin-screw 40-foot express cruiser, isn't there. She is in a culdesac on the upwind side of the long leg of the wharf before it shapes out into a T. A strong current sucking under the wharf is not breasting us away from it. On the contrary. Oh, definitely, on the contrary. Those scrunching noises are caused by our white topsides rubbing on the tarred piles of the wharf.

On the way in to the pier the afternoon before, the crewman who had been standing by the anchor while we were making up our minds, accidentally let it slip overboard about twenty-five yards off. He paid the cable out and secured the slack end of it to the windlass but didn't mention it until we were safely moored with four lines out to bollards on the wharf. As it was then time for cocktails we left the anchor where it was.

So much for background. We now see how to get away from the wharf in the teeth of the howling northeaster. We ask kind strangers to let go our lines—which are not needed anyway—and the crewman heaves around on the windlass while we go ahead with the inboard propeller and astern with the other. All shipshape and Bristol fashion, as the saying is.

Just then we notice that a large, tremendously powerful converted trawler which had anchored farther out during the night has dragged down on top of our anchor. Our horn attracts no signs of life on the trawler. We think she should get out of our way before we run into her with our knife-edge bow and perhaps cut her in half.

We had not previously noted that the kind stranger who let go our after spring line tossed it into the water instead of on to our deck. It wraps itself around our port propeller and stops the motor.

With icy calm—no screaming and only a little jumping up and down—we stop the other motor just before it sucks us under the impressive bowsprit of a large schooner moored directly astern. The captain and crew of the schooner are much interested in the solution of our problem. Although we cannot hear their words we see their mouths going.

To shame them we light a cigarette, pull our sou-wester firmly over our ears, swallow our Adam's apple and step out of our snug wheelhouse into the howling wind and rain—with some snow. We look to windward at the dragging trawler and see a large smoke ring emerging from her vertical exhaust stack. It is followed by others in rapidly increasing succession and the trawler moves ahead, dragging her anchor and ours which is afoul of it. Perforce we leave the wharf, the schooner and all our other troubles astern of us.

Presently when there is plenty of sea room the trawler stops puffing. A man appears on deck huddled against the wind and

snow—and a little sleet—and gives his anchor cable more scope so that she will not drag again. We follow suit and all hands go below for another rubber of bridge.

"If you want a nice cold drink, just say so."

Fouled painter

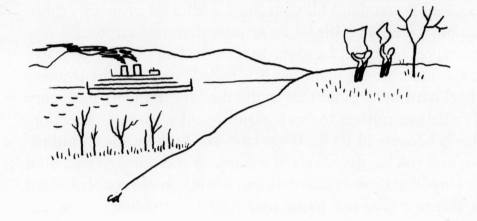

The Compass

THE COMPASS

Although the magnetic compass is a north-seeking device having a card inscribed with the initial letters of 31 of the 32 points it does not give you an N for North. This seemingly flattering presumption that you know where North is derives from the fact that when the Chinese Communists discovered the compass centuries ago they were unlettered.

Steering a boat by compass is a knack which is easily acquired if you don't fill your head with a lot of useless information. To begin with let us assume that you are under way in a motor boat that happens to have a compass. Fix your eye on the Fleur-de-lys point (as it is called) and put the steering wheel hard over. Note that while the boat remains stationary the compass appears to rotate rapidly in the opposite direction. This is because of its north-seeking attribute and is an indication that you have confused the compass and not yourself. If an anchored boat comes into collision while you are concentrating on this test take her name and report the owner to the authorities.

If you are steering the boat on a straight course you will very soon see that the compass wants to deviate to one side or the other. This is what is known as compass deviation. To correct it change course very slightly in the opposite direction. If that doesn't work try it the proper way. The more you deviate the farther you go and the more fun you have steering.

Modern charts give courses based on true North, which in different parts of the earth varies with relation to the magnetic pole. This variation is called variation and it is necessary to correct for it. Correct-right-east is a phrase which helps people to remember whether easterly variation should be corrected to the right or to the left. Or, as we nauticians say, to port or star-

board. The gimmick is to remember whether you are correcting from true to compass or from compass to true.

See?

The Glasses

THE GLASSES

You might think from the foregoing that when a yachtsman asked you for the glasses you should be expected to hand him two or three barometers. This is not the case. The glasses, as any dope should know, are actually the binoculars.

On a well appointed yacht there are several pairs of glasses. There is the pair that was received as a prize in a race many years ago. Second prize, second-rate glasses. In use, they confirm the buoy or prominent headland that you have already seen with the naked eye, merely dimming the image slightly.

There is also the battered pair that was picked up on a battle-field in one war or another. Being of small, handy size, they lie around on deck where people sit on them and say, "Ouch!" If a guest tries to use them he blinks and says, "My, the sights those glasses must have seen." Unfortunately, they don't see good any more.

Then, in addition to the fine glasses that guests bring aboard and stingily stash away for their own use, there is the pair that belongs exclusively to the skipper. He sets them to his own eyes so that he will not lose valuable moments focusing them when a pretty girl passes by in another boat. Being very polite he says, "These are my own Seven Fifties. Use them if you have to, but remember they're mine."

To make sure they remember he keeps his glasses in a beautiful little water-tight mahogany box with hinged lid near the steering wheel. The box is water-tight in the sense that when rain or spray gets in it does not leak out.

Some very intelligent skippers mount the box so that the opening is not on top but on one side. This keeps the water from getting in the top. An added advantage is that when it gets in the side it runs out pretty soon. When the boat is knocked down by a sudden gust of wind the glasses float out. After this has happened a few times anybody is welcome to use them.

In almost any crew there is some young lad with good eyes who can alert the skipper when there are quail in sight.

U.S.P.S. MANNERS AND CUSTOMS: "The only piece of
nautical wearing apparel that is usually worn by the
small boat owner is the yachting cap."

"I think the poor girl's lost her Bikini. . . .

Shall I get the binoculars?"

The Glass

THE GLASS

The barometer is an instrument which for some obscure reason is called a glass.

If you are cruising aboard a friend's boat and want to be thought salty you should ask him bright and early in the morning, "What's the glass doing?"

He will thereupon step over to the barometer which is securely fastened to a wall that he calls a bulkhead and say, "My God, the bottom has fallen out of it!"

Before you have time to offer to sweep it up he will add, "That settles it, we won't turn a wheel today."

Looking carefully at the glass you will observe that over to the right it says "Very dry." If you say these words aloud once or twice your host will be reminded of his duties and you won't have to wait until the sun is over the yardarm.

There are days when the bottom has not fallen out of the glass and when the yachtsman has to tap it to see whether the little black hand moves up or down. He then says, "Mmm, that's what I was afraid of."

Pressed for an explanation he will continue, "Well, the weather picture has been rather striated for several days with highs and lows stationary or moving rapidly out to sea along the St. Lawrence River Valley. If you want my candid opinion we'll sit tight today."

In reply to that dismal foreboding you may, if you want, say "Very dry."

Of course, the situation is further complicated by the fact that atmospheric pressure is no longer measured in inches but in millibars. If I tell you that a millibar "is a unit of measure of atmospheric pressure, equal to one thousand dynes per square centimeter" you will understand why the weather has been so unsettled lately.

In addition to the glass for casual reference and tapping purposes the really expert yachtsman has on his boat a barograph called a barograph. This has a revolving barrel on which a stylus draws the vagaries of the millibars in blue ink. It has to be wound up and a new paper wrapped around the barrel once a week, but isn't. The stylus is not supposed to make blotches on the paper, but does. Once in a long while when everything is working the inked line shows a series of squiggles with a pronounced V in between. When this happens the paper is removed from the barograph, straightened out and tacked to the bulkhead. Ever after the yachtsman fortunate enough to own one of these priceless records points it out to guests and says, "That's the day the bottom fell out of the glass, and were we lucky not to be at sea somewhere!"

The only other thing to know about a barometer is that it makes a handy hat rack. If you hang your hat over it you can get in some wonderful cruising without having the pants scared off you.

Women's Wear

WOMEN'S WEAR

Some girls who are invited out for a sail for the first time think they can make a hit by wearing patched blue jeans and a blouse and taking along a fetching Bikini suit. Nothing could be farther from the truth. Yachtsmen are great sticklers for propriety and like their guests to come aboard with clothes for every occasion. So if you have been invited aboard a 26-footer for a week-end cruise wear a smart suit and pack your things in two or three large suitcases. When you get aboard just pitch right in and put your gear in any lockers that you find empty. Ask your host to stow the suitcases in the trunk rack which is provided for that purpose, and he will be delighted also to assign you a hanging locker for your party dresses and furs.

You have probably been advised not to wear high heel shoes, and I have seen many inexperienced girls go through the embarrassing routine of removing their shoes and stepping aboard in their stocking feet. Those that had stockings, I mean. The important thing is to be sure that there are no protruding nails in the shoes, and the way to verify this is to spin around first on one foot and then the other on any varnished surface. The main hatch cover is almost always varnished. No marks, no nails—and even if there are a few circular scratches they may have been caused by oily pepples adhering to your shoes.

"It doesn't seem to want to come off."

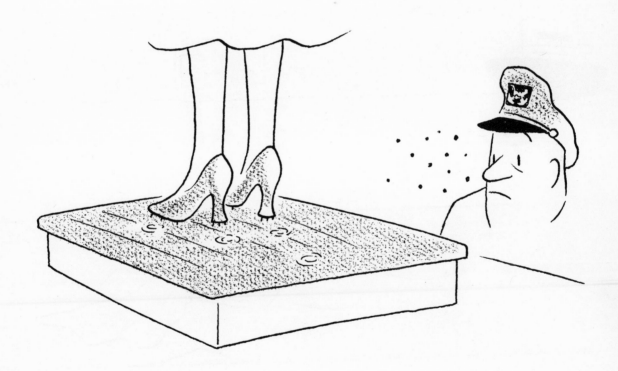

The Eight-Sevenths Rule

THE EIGHT-SEVENTHS RULE

I happened to find a pamphlet issued by the Navy in war time and addressed to officers who had been assigned to duty in mine craft. It was marked Confidential, but across the top of it in hand-writing which was not that of the Secretary of the Navy was the word Declassified and so I trust I am not violating security in quoting a short paragraph of instructions, namely:

"Have all departments assembled and try out all gear where possible, such as anchors, chains, boat gear, etc. Be sure and check thoroughly all navigational equipment: compasses, pelorus, sextants, chronometers, stadiometer, etc."

If these precepts were observed in these piping times of peace by pleasure boaters there wouldn't be the terrific crowding there is on the waterways. People would spend half their free time finding and assembling departments (if any) and the other half checking gear and navigational instruments.

However, we have to take the rough with the smooth and my next precept is from a popular book on cruising. (Not the one I wrote, which is out of print.) It is assumed that a man and his party have gone off on a long cruise without having checked navigational instruments and that Washington Monument is suddenly sighted dead ahead. Our skipper has remembered since boyhood days that the monument is 555 feet high and to find out how far removed from it he is he applies the 8/7ths rule. To avoid inaccuracy he applies the rule also to the lesser height of his own eye above sea level, which we may assume to be nine feet. That's it—he's 30.5 nautical miles away. A simple way of expressing the formula is: D (miles) = 1 1/7 h (feet), where D is distance and h is the height of the object above sea level.

So far he knows his distance from the monument without knowing his actual position, but this problem is quickly solved. Converting sea miles to land miles in his head, he picks up a road map of Maryland, Virginia, the District of Columbia and part of Pennsylvania and steps off his distance from the monument. If the water is a deep chocolate color he is in the Potomac River, headed approximately north. But if it is any other color he is in Chesapeake Bay, probably headed west. In either case he will be aground in a few seconds.

This contretemps is what the Navy had in mind when it said to try out anchors, chains, boat gear, etc., when possible.

"If you ask me, I think we're off the Virgin Islands."

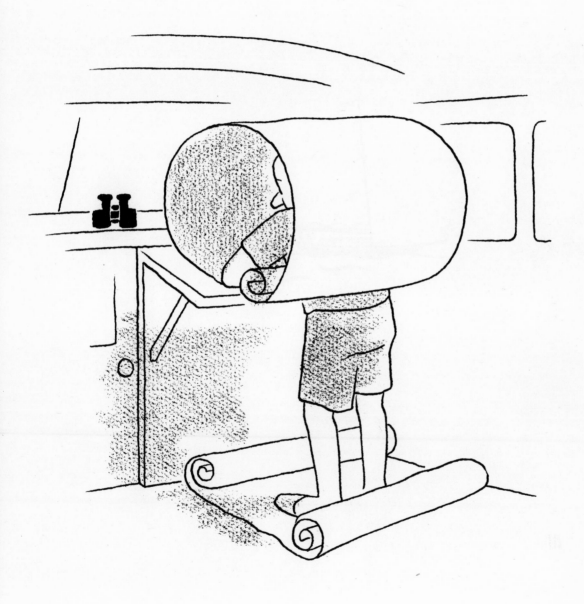

Of charts. . . .

Bow and Beam Bearings

BOW AND BEAM BEARINGS

Needless to say, it is not always possible to check your position by the 8/7ths rule and the known height of Washington Monument, and it is therefore important for the tyro to memorize the heights of other edifices—such as the Empire State Building or the Taj Mahal.

If you are not cruising in either of these vicinities it is still possible to find your position by a method known as taking bow and beam bearings. An unthinking landlubber might think that a bow bearing is one taken dead ahead and an ignoramus would be sure to think it to be the foremost crankshaft bearing in his motor. As we know very well, however, a bow bearing is one taken by compass or pelorus when an object bears four points or 45 degrees from the bow. Nothing could be simpler and either bow will do, according to where we find the object.

Let us assume we are approaching a point of land off which lies a dangerous rocky reef. We are going at flank speed of 30 knots and although we are consuming 30 gallons of gasoline an hour at 30 cents a gallon these elements do not figure in our equation. (They are useful, however, as an entertainment item in our tax deductions.) When the point of land is broad on the bow (another way of saying it is 45 degrees or four points off the bow) we start our stop watch if we have one or stop it if we didn't know it was already running.

Exactly four minutes later (for the sake of the example) we observe that the point of land is broad abeam—which is to say that it's right out there, sideways. In those four minutes we have covered two miles and we are therefore two miles off the point. If the rocky shoal extends more than two miles off the point we've had it.

In this case we just activate our ship-to-shore phone (if it is still activatable) and ask the Marine Operator to give us our insurance company.

"Wasn't that a taxi that just passed us?"

"Oops!"

Doubling the Angle on the Bow

DOUBLING THE ANGLE ON THE BOW

Because of the risk inherent in the foregoing example careful navigators like to know how far off a point of land or other prominent object they will be before they come to it. They accomplish their meticulous object by a parlay known as doubling the angle on the bow.

First catch your navigator. In the old days this could be done with any spirits of alcohol except methylated. Now that navigators are a dime a dozen they are more choosy and have to be lured with fair promises of French wines, delicious viands, comfortable sleeping quarters, ample sleeping time and no extra-curricular duties. In a sail boat, for example, it is unthinkable that a navigator should be asked to turn to and set sail or handle sheets with the common ordinary run of guests. If he is asked to he will at once produce his navigator's workbook and, if at sea, rework a few day-old sights. If in waters subject to the inland rules of the road and the AAU he will double the angle on the bow.

If a navigator is asked the position of the boat which he is navigating he will resort to the time-honored witticism of laying the palm of his hand on a chart and saying, "Right here." If his host—who, after all, owns the boat and is keeping the navigator in food and drink—asks how many miles remain in the course of a day's run the expert will tell him that if he were only left alone for a few minutes he would be able to figure it out. If you ask him to lend the cook a hand washing up he will not only double the angle on the bow but turn himself inside out.

So we might as well learn how it is done. We sight the prominent object somewhere and when it is, say, 23½ degrees from the bow we note the time. Then when the angle is twice 23½ degrees or 47 we read the time again and the distance run between bearings is equal to the distance that we'll be away from the prominent object when it is abeam.

This is expressed in the trigonometric equation—

$$PAO = 180° - (POA + APO)$$
$$= 180° - (\alpha + 180° - 2\alpha)$$
$$= \alpha.$$

Of course, you have to have a diagram and to know what all those letters, including the cute little Greek *alpha*, stand for—which I don't.

Perhaps it is better to steer for the buoy since that is why it's there.

"He's Going out on deck. to take bearings, whatever they are."

"Do you have a bromo on you?"

One-Design Class Racing

Signaling

"What's a good name?"

"Okay there, Gallagher . . . I'm wise to you!"

Motor Boat Racing

MOTOR BOAT RACING

Motor boat racing is totally different from the slow-motion pastime engaged in by the sail boat fanatics. In the former sport the fastest boat so frequently wins that she is (or they are) deceptively named Slo-Mo-Shun. We shall therefore not concern ourselves with this exclusive phenomenon but with a subsidiary branch called Predicted Log Racing.

On board ship, as we all know, there are three logs and generally no fireplace. The shaft log is the only one of the three that is contrived from wood, and even that is sometimes iron or bronze. Then there is the taffrail log which is always bronze or some cheap substitute and which is towed from the taffrail. There are several rails on a boat but only one taffrail. At the inboard end of the towed line there is a dial with a pointer on it which counts the passing miles, thus rendering it unnecessary to go overboard and drift astern on the log line to get a reading. Some fancy logs, come to think of it, are designed with the dial integral with the rotor which is towed astern, and I suppose in that case you do have to go overboard.

Finally, we have the log itself. You have to know what this is so that when the skipper says, "Read the log and enter the reading in the log" you'll know what he is talking about. The log, therefore, is a book having columns on its pages where entries may be made. It is also used for unlikely autographs, merry wit and poisonous poetry.

The Predicted Log Race stems from this. The owner of a 12-knot family cruiser keeps book on the time it takes him to go from here to there, noting carefully in the log distances, the state of the current and the times of passing various points. The owner of a high-speed runabout does the same in half the time and somewhat more than twice the informality. Owners of slow buckets get a pretty good idea of how long it will take them to pass a given spot if the spot is stationary, and presently the yacht club to which all belong runs a Predicted Log Race.

In this, each competitor estimates how long it will take him to go around a dog-legged course and at what instant he will pass each of several stipulated control points. Boy oh boy, does he put himself out on a limb, because when the race starts he finds on board an unwelcome guest who collects all watches belonging to owner and crew and stops the clock with a powerful magnet. He has a watch of his own and at each control point he peaks at it and surreptitiously makes an entry in his own diary. We can only hope that while observing the performance of our boat he is not betting on that of a competitor.

But we give him the benefit of the doubt and the race is run, and nobody knows who won until days later when the last boat is in. And she wins if her owner happened to guess his finish time correctly and most accurately predict his arrival time at every control point. If he'd had a little inconspicuous watch not belonging to himself or any member of his crew and had consulted it unobtrusively from time to time, his predictions would have been 100% correct and he would have won a gold-plated aneroid thermometer. But one can't hope for everything in this vale of tears.

"See . . . you drive it just like a car."

Outboard Runabouts

OUTBOARD RUNABOUTS

It should not be rashly assumed from the foregoing that there are no longer outboard motors of the type that one clamps to the sterns of runabouts and hydroplanes. There are, in point of fact, hundreds of thousands of them in our harbors and accessible waterways, and the beauty of them is that by common decree of the manufacturers they have been completely silenced. That combination of excruciating noises that used to be heard—eeeg-unk, whee-blunk, eeii-guk, blop—now emanates from earth-moving equipment more than a mile away. The next step in the advance of science will be the elimination of bulldozers.

With the reduction of outboards to whispering silence much picturesque speech has departed from the yachting scene. Until recently, you and your lovely bride would have been sailing quietly about your business when an outboard darted past you at 20 miles an hour, its occupants unaware that their voices could be heard above the weeii-glink, miiee-munk of motor and boat.

One occupant would have said, "I'll buy that bleach blonde in the shorts and bra," and another would have retorted, "That babe's old enough to be your grandmother." The boat would have been out of gunshot before you could have taken defensive action.

That and much more like it has been regrettably lost. With stillness has come courtesy and if anybody half encircles you at high speed he almost invariably completes the circle to see what damage has been done. Outboardists go miles out of their way to avoid interfering with a sail boat race, and those who tow beautiful dolls on water skis choose the least frequented waterways.

Fortunately for all concerned the operation of outboard motor boats is as simple as tight-rope walking. A man on a taut wire over a river gorge is not required to learn anything about rules of the road or navigational aids. Buoys don't confuse him. Meeting and crossing situations are unknown and rocks never rise up from the bottom to impede his progress. So it is also with outboarders. If a man can drive a car and signal right or left turns without an electric turning indicator he is an expert water cowboy. Older and more cautious forms of marine life instinctively avoid him.

"For a moment there, I thought that was your mother . . . but she has more mustache."

"I don't like the looks of things."

"Get lost, Simpkins!"

Weather Forecasting

WEATHER FORECASTING

In ye olden days before the establishment of the Weather Bureau and the invention of radio, seafarers used to cover quite amazing distances in safety as a result of analyzing the portents of the sky. Superstition was part of it, but they learned simple little jingles at their mothers' knees and were wont to recite them—spout were the better word—*was* a better word, I mean —at the slightest provocation. For example:

> "A red sky in the morning
> Is the sailor's warning.
> A red sky at night
> Is the sailor's delight."

I don't know whether they actually got up at sun up to see whether the sky was red and streaky and wicked looking, but if they didn't, labor was so cheap in those days that they could hire a man to do it for them. In the evening toward the end of the second dog watch (the traditional time for watching the two canine mascots romp on deck) the captain himself would look at the sky and if it was red he predicted that the next day would be fair—or at least fair to middling—and that he could sleep hearty all night.

Sometimes the captain would delegate the first mate to rouse himself out shortly after the hypothetical time of sunrise and if he saw a bank of low clouds fringing the horizon to eastward he would call it a "high dawn" and make all necessary preparations for blowing weather. But on the other hand if there was rain before seven the captain knew that that rhymed with "clear before eleven" and anticipated a pleasant afternoon. The change from God's time to daylight saving time has ruined that jingle, however.

Then there was one that ran:

> "When the glass falls low,
> Prepare for a blow;
> When it rises high
> Let all your kites fly."

Although kite-flying is now a sport for kids, Benjamin Franklin at one time thought quite highly of it, and I suppose that is why the allusion got into the jingle. The oldtime skippers exercised some discrimination, however (this was before discrimination became a penal offense) and bore it in mind that:

> "First rise after low,
> Indicates a stronger blow."

In that case I assume that the hard-bitten skipper of ye olden times would stay below and play mumbletypeg on the cabin table instead of flying his kites. But he would never stick his knife into the forward side of the mainmast as that was a sure way of bringing wind.

One more quotation from the classics before we close this instructive dissertation on outmoded weather forecasting. Years ago before the millibars confused the weather picture there was the saying:

> "When the rain's before the wind
> Halliards, sheets and braces mind.
> But when the wind's before the rain
> Let your topsails draw again."

You get the meaning of this if you remember that at one time "wind" rhymed with "kind" and that "rain" rhymed with "then." Seafarers no longer wear braces—except young female ones on their front teeth.

Of what use is all this silly lore to modern sailors? None whatever. If you turn out in the morning and find the radio

busted; if you then tap the glass and the hand shows no movement in either direction, row right ashore and phone the Weather Bureau for instructions. Don't look at the sky on the way in. You'd only be confused.

"Now, you all can swim, I presume."

CONCLUSION

So many admirable books have been written on the aquatic sport of kings and their glamorous queens that I am surprised it ever occurred to any one that I could write another one. However, it's done now, and as the fellow said, there's no use crying over spilt milk.

What I have tried to point out is that at sea in small boats eternal vigilance is the price of . . . Well, we'll skip it as I've forgotten what it's of. Probably a book.

If in the foregoing chapters some of my words haven't seemed to make sense try translating them into your favorite foreign language. Backwards. Then sing them.